Thomas Hardy: The Novels

ANALYSING TEXTS

General Editor: Nicholas Marsh

Chaucer: *The Canterbury Tales*   *Gail Ashton*

Webster: The Tragedies   *Kate Aughterson*

Shakespeare: The Comedies   *R. P. Draper*

Charlotte Brontë: The Novels   *Mike Edwards*

Shakespeare: The Tragedies   *Nicholas Marsh*

Jane Austen: The Novels   *Nicholas Marsh*

Emily Brontë: *Wuthering Heights*   *Nicholas Marsh*

Virginia Woolf: The Novels   *Nicholas Marsh*

D. H. Lawrence: The Novels   *Nicholas Marsh*

John Donne: The Poems   *Joe Nutt*

Thomas Hardy: The Novels   *Norman Page*

Analysing Texts
Series Standing Order ISBN 0–333–73260–X
(*outside North America only*)

You can receive future titles in this series as they are published by placing a standing order. Please contact your bookseller or, in the case of difficulty, write to us at the address below with your name and address, the title of the series and the ISBN quoted above.

Customer Services Department, Macmillan Distribution Ltd
Houndmills, Basingstoke, Hampshire RG21 6XS, England

Thomas Hardy: The Novels

NORMAN PAGE

palgrave

First published 2001 by
PALGRAVE
Houndmills, Basingstoke, Hampshire RG21 6XS and
175 Fifth Avenue, New York, N.Y. 10010
Companies and representatives throughout the world

PALGRAVE is the new global academic imprint of St. Martin's Press LLC
Scholarly and Reference Division and Palgrave Publishers Ltd (formerly
Macmillan Press Ltd).

ISBN 0–333–91436–8 hardback
ISBN 0–333–71617–5 paperback

This book is printed on paper suitable for recycling and
made from fully managed and sustained forest sources.

A catalogue record for this book is available
from the British Library.

Library of Congress Cataloging-in-Publication Data
Page, Norman.
    Thomas Hardy : the novels / Norman Page.
        p. cm. — (Analysing texts)
    Includes bibliographical references and index.
    ISBN 0–333–91436–8 (cloth) — ISBN 0–333–71617–5 (pbk.)
    1. Hardy, Thomas, 1840–1928—Fictional works. 2. Wessex
(England)—In literature. I. Title. II. Series.

PR4757.F5 .P34 2000
823'.8—dc21
                                                            00–048310

10   9   8   7   6   5   4   3   2   1
10   09 08 07 06 05 04 03 02 01
Printed in China

For Edward Hughes

Contents

General Editor's Preface   viii

PART 1: THE NOVELS

Introduction   3

1   Writer and Reader   **4**
   Introduction   4
   The Mayor of Casterbridge and the Voice of the
     Hardyan Narrator   6
   Jude the Obscure: Dramatic Method   11
   Tess of the d'Urbervilles: the Narrative of Indirection 16
   Far from the Madding Crowd and Psychological Analysis   21
   Conclusions   27
   Methods of Analysis   28
   Suggestions for Further Work   29

2   Beginnings and Endings   **30**
   Introduction   30
   The Mayor of Casterbridge: a Family without a Name   32
   Far from the Madding Crowd: a 'rural painting'   40
   Jude the Obscure: the Uses of Realism   45
   Tess of the d'Urbervilles: the Case of the Disappearing
     Heroine   51
   Conclusions   56
   Methods of Analysis   57
   Suggestions for Further Work   57

3   Nature and Humanity   **59**
   Introduction   59
   Tess of the d'Urbervilles: 'impregnated by their
     surroundings'   60

Jude the Obscure: Landscape and Alienation   65
Far from the Madding Crowd: Nature's Violence   71
The Mayor of Casterbridge: the Uncertainty of Harvests   74
Conclusions   79
Methods of Analysis   82
Suggestions for Further Work   83

4 Individuals and Communities   **84**
Introduction   84
Far from the Madding Crowd: 'in harmony'   85
Tess of the d'Urbervilles: the 'club-walking'   91
Jude the Obscure: the Outsider   96
The Mayor of Casterbridge: Communal Punishment   100
Conclusions   105
Methods of Analysis   106
Suggestions for Further Work   107

5 Tradition and Change   **108**
Introduction   108
Tess of the d'Urbervilles: the Two Worlds of
    Country and City   108
Jude the Obscure: Change in the Village   113
The Mayor of Casterbridge: the Mechanization of Farming   117
Far from the Madding Crowd: the Woman Farmer   122
Conclusions   127
Methods of Analysis   127
Suggestions for Further Work   128

6 Men and Women   **130**
Introduction   130
Far from the Madding Crowd: a Symbolic Seduction   131
Jude the Obscure: Male Innocence and Female Designs   136
The Mayor of Casterbridge: Love and Rivalry   142
Tess of the d'Urbervilles: Ideal and Reality in Love   147
Conclusions   153
Methods of Analysis   156
Suggestions for Further Work   156

PART 2: THE CONTEXT

7   Hardy's Life and Work   161

8   The Context of Hardy's Fiction   174

9   Samples of Criticism   183
     Michael Millgate, *Thomas Hardy: His Career
         as a Novelist* (1971)   183
     Arnold Kettle, *'Tess of the d'Urbervilles'* (1951)   185
     Rosemarie Morgan, *Cancelled Words: Rediscovering
         Thomas Hardy* (1992)   188
     Elaine Showalter, 'The Unmanning of the Mayor
         of Casterbridge' (1979)   190
     Richard Dellamora, *Masculine Desire: The Sexual
         Politics of Victorian Aestheticism* (1990)   192

10 Guide to Further Reading   194
     Autobiography and Biography   194
     Reference   195
     Criticism: General   195
     Criticism: Specific Texts   196

Index   198

General Editor's Preface

This series is dedicated to one clear belief: that we can all enjoy, understand and analyse literature for ourselves, provided we know how to do it. How can we build on close understanding of a short passage, and develop our insight into the whole work? What features do we expect to find in a text? Why do we study style in so much detail? In demystifying the study of literature, these are only some of the questions the *Analysing Texts* series addresses and answers.

The books in this series will not do all the work for you, but will provide you with the tools, and show you how to use them. Here, you will find samples of close, detailed analysis, with an explanation of the analytical techniques utilized. At the end of each chapter there are useful suggestions for further work you can do to practise, develop and hone the skills demonstrated and build confidence in your own analytical ability.

An author's individuality shows in the way they write: every work they produce bears the hallmark of that writer's personal 'style'. In the main part of each book we concentrate therefore on analysing the particular flavour and concerns of one author's work, and explain the features of their writing in connection with major themes. In Part 2 there are chapters about the author's life and work, assessing their contribution to developments in literature; and a sample of critics' views are summarized and discussed in comparison with each other. Some suggestions for further reading provide a bridge towards further critical research.

Analysing Texts is designed to stimulate and encourage your critical and analytic faculty, to develop your personal insight into the author's work and individual style, and to provide you with the skills and techniques to enjoy at first hand the excitement of discovering the richness of the text.

NICHOLAS MARSH

PART 1

THE NOVELS

Introduction

Hardy published fourteen novels, and this book is primarily concerned with four of them – though it should be said that many of the
points made apply also to works not directly discussed here. In the
first six chapters, the four texts will be considered from different
points of view so as to illuminate various aspects of theme, ideas,
style and technique. In each chapter, passages from the four novels
will be used as starting-points. The analyses of these passages will
draw attention to specific features that are characteristic of the text in
question or, in many cases, of Hardy's fiction as a whole. In this way,
detailed analysis will often broaden into generalization, and at the end
of each chapter there are suggestions of other passages that the
student may wish to subject to similar analysis.

1

Writer and Reader

Introduction

Hardy grew up in a culture in which storytelling, especially by word of mouth, was a normal part of the pattern of daily life: from his grandmother, for example, who lived with the Hardy family for many years, he heard stories of the time before his own birth, and the ballads and songs of the region were another kind of narrative art with which he became familiar from his earliest years. On a different level, he acquired a close knowledge of the stories told in the Bible, and as soon as he could read his mother gave him books that included some of the popular novelists of the day as well as more serious fare.

It is not surprising, therefore, that the basis of Hardy's art as a novelist should be the ancient role of the storyteller. But by the time he entertained ambitions to be a novelist, the English novel had reached a considerable degree of maturity and technical sophistication. The earlier traditions represented by such authors as Henry Fielding and Jane Austen, and the more recent achievements of (among many others) Charles Dickens and George Eliot, had created a genre that appealed to very large audiences and that had brought the primitive act of storytelling to a new pitch of complexity and subtlety. In material terms, it had also proved capable of making authors and their publishers rich: Dickens and George Eliot (both, like Hardy, from humble backgrounds) had made fortunes from their books, and Hardy in turn was to die a very wealthy man.

Reading Hardy's novels, we become aware of the ways in which he conceived and defined his own role as storyteller. To a very important extent, these were influenced by the prevailing modes of publication – the distinctive methods by which fiction was marketed in the mid and late-Victorian period – and more will be said on this subject in a later chapter. For the moment it needs to be stressed that if Hardy had been writing at any other time he might have written novels of a very different kind, and of course the same is true of other writers of the period. Ultimately it was the constraints put upon the writer's freedom by the commercial aspect of novel-writing that contributed largely to his abandoning of fiction in favour of poetry, which offered the writer a much greater degree of personal freedom. But for nearly thirty years Hardy pursued the novelist's trade, and part of the interest in reading his work lies in considering how far he succeeded in effecting a compromise between what the genre and the market demanded and what he personally wished to express and explore. For, while his novels are in some respects representative examples of late nineteenth-century fiction, they are also in other ways, and on every page, uniquely and unmistakably Hardyan.

Anyone writing a novel has to make certain choices and decisions at the outset, concerning such matters as narrative point of view, the handling of time, the presentation of character, the use of settings, and so forth. In this chapter we shall consider extracts that exemplify the ways in which Hardy responded to some of these challenges. In deciding on a narrative point of view, for example, he is both conservative and highly original. All his novels use a third-person narrator: there is nothing resembling Charlotte Brontë's *Jane Eyre* or Dickens's *Great Expectations*, in which the protagonist tells her or his own story, and certainly nothing like Emily Brontë's *Wuthering Heights* or Wilkie Collins's *The Woman in White*, with their complex interweaving of first-person narratives. But within this traditional format, Hardy produces many original and distinctive effects, and the 'voice' of his narrators, those important though often elusive figures through whom the writer communicates with the reader, is not always easy to define. Related to this is the writer's awareness of his audience and the kind of readers of which it

consisted. This and other questions will be raised by the passages that
follow.

The Mayor of Casterbridge and the Voice of the Hardyan Narrator

In the following extract, the narrative voice can fairly easily be
defined:

> The Ring at Casterbridge was merely the local name of one of the
> finest Roman Amphitheatres, if not the very finest, remaining in
> Britain.
>
> Casterbridge announced old Rome in every street, alley, and pre-
> cinct. It looked Roman, bespoke the art of Rome, concealed dead men
> of Rome. It was impossible to dig more than a foot or two deep about
> the town fields and gardens without coming upon some tall soldier or
> other of the Empire, who had lain there in his silent unobtrusive rest
> for a space of fifteen hundred years. He was mostly found lying on his
> side, in an oval scoop in the chalk, like a chicken in its shell; his knees
> drawn up to his chest; sometimes with the remains of his spear against
> his arm; a fibula or brooch of bronze on his breast or forehead; an urn
> at his knees, a jar at his throat, a bottle at his mouth; and mystified
> conjecture pouring down upon him from the eyes of Casterbridge
> street boys and men, who had turned a moment to gaze at the familiar
> spectacle as they passed by.
>
> Imaginative inhabitants, who would have felt an unpleasantness at
> the discovery of a comparatively modern skeleton in their gardens,
> were quite unmoved by these hoary shapes. They had lived so long
> ago, their time was so unlike the present, their hopes and motives were
> so widely removed from ours, that between them and the living there
> seemed to stretch a gulf too wide for even a spirit to pass.
>
> The Amphitheatre was a huge circular enclosure, with a notch at
> opposite extremities of its diameter north and south. From its sloping
> internal form it might have been called the spittoon of the Jötuns. It was
> to Casterbridge what the ruined Coliseum is to modern Rome, and was
> nearly of the same magnitude. The dusk of evening was the proper hour
> at which a true impression of this suggestive place could be received.
> Standing in the middle of the arena at that time there by degrees became

apparent its real vastness, which a cursory view from the summit at noon-day was apt to obscure. Melancholy, impressive, lonely, yet accessible from every part of the town, the historic circle was the frequent spot for appointments of a furtive kind. Intrigues were arranged there; tentative meetings were there experimented after divisions and feuds. But one kind of appointment – in itself the most common of any – seldom had place in the Amphitheatre: that of happy lovers.

Why, seeing that it was pre-eminently an airy, accessible, and sequestered spot for interviews, the cheerfullest form of those occurrences never took kindly to the soil of the ruin, would be a curious inquiry. Perhaps it was because its associations had about them something sinister. Its history proved that. Apart from the sanguinary nature of the games originally played therein, such incidents attached to its past as these: that for scores of years the town-gallows had stood at one corner; that in 1705 a woman who had murdered her husband was half-strangled and then burnt there in the presence of ten thousand spectators. Tradition reports that at a certain stage of the burning her heart burst and leapt out of her body, to the terror of them all, and that not one of those ten thousand people ever cared particularly for hot roast after that. In addition to these old tragedies, pugilistic encounters almost to the death had come off down to recent dates in that secluded arena, entirely invisible to the outside world save by climbing to the top of the enclosure, which few townspeople in the daily round of their lives ever took the trouble to do. So that, though close to the turnpike-road, crimes might be perpetrated there unseen at mid-day.

Some boys had latterly tried to impart gaiety to the ruin by using the central arena as a cricket-ground. But the game usually languished for the aforesaid reason – the dismal privacy which the earthen circle enforced, shutting out every appreciative passer's vision, every commendatory remark from outsiders – everything, except the sky; and to play at games in such circumstances was like acting to an empty house. Possibly, too, the boys were timid, for some old people said that at certain moments in the summer time, in broad daylight, persons sitting with a book or dozing in the arena had, on lifting their eyes, beheld the slopes lined with a gazing legion of Hadrian's soldiery as if watching the gladiatorial combat; and had heard the roar of their excited voices; that the scene would remain but a moment, like a lightning flash, and then disappear.

It was related that there still remained under the south entrance excavated cells for the reception of the wild animals and athletes who

took part in the games. The arena was still smooth and circular, as if
used for its original purpose not so very long ago. The sloping pathways by which spectators had ascended to their seats were pathways
yet. But the whole was grown over with grass, which now, at the end of
summer, was bearded with withered bents that formed waves under
the brush of the wind, returning to the attentive ear Aeolian modulations, and detaining for moments the flying globes of thistledown.

Henchard had chosen this spot as being the safest from observation
which he could think of for meeting his long-lost wife, and at the same
time as one easily to be found by a stranger after nightfall. As Mayor of
the town, with a reputation to keep up, he could not invite her to come
to his house till some definite course had been decided on.

(Chapter 11)

This is a passage wholly dominated by the narrative voice: not a
single word of dialogue (that is, speech uttered by one of the
characters in the story) is introduced. It has, indeed, something of
the flavour of an essay or article, and it is only at the very end, when
the name of Henchard is introduced, that it clearly emerges as part of
a work of fiction. At first glance, therefore, one might be inclined
to dismiss it as a kind of mini-essay introduced into the text of the
novel, perhaps as padding. But closer examination reveals that there
is some interesting variety even within the prevailing non-fictional
material.

What characteristics can be attributed to the narrator – the storyteller whose 'voice' addresses us; and what can be learned about the
implied readers of such a passage? The primary subject of the passage
is the evidence still to be seen, in the area in question, of the Roman
occupation of Britain, and in particular an important historical site on
the outskirts of the fictional town of Casterbridge; but many readers,
especially those familiar with the south-west of England and with
Hardy's earlier novels, would have had little difficulty in identifying
Casterbridge with Dorchester (known as Durnovaria to the Roman
settlers), and 'the Ring' with Maumbury Rings, a site on the edge of
Dorchester containing the ruins of a Roman amphitheatre. The narrator is knowledgeable on the subject of local history and archaeology,
and at first adopts the detached manner of one writing a guidebook or
popular history. When a specialized term is used, its meaning is

explained, on the implicit assumption that the reader is not an expert on the subject and may need a little help: 'a fibula or brooch of bronze'.

Soon, however, a more personal note intrudes: the description of the skeleton of a Roman soldier in its grave is detailed and precise, but there is a rhetorical and even a poetic, rather than an objective and scientific, note in the reference to the body having lain for 1500 years 'in his silent unobtrusive rest'. Precision and objectivity, again, mark the opening sentence of the fourth paragraph quoted, with its indications of the amphitheatre's main physical features; but here, too, a poetic note is heard in the description of the scene at dusk, 'Melancholy, impressive, lonely', which would have been somewhat out of place in, say, an article in a journal devoted to local history or archaeology. A little later, the reference to a public execution in 1705 shows not the cool, dispassionate manner of the historian but a curious mixture of genuine horror ('her heart burst and leapt out of her body') and grim facetiousness ('ever cared particularly for hot roast...' is likely to strike us as a distinctly 'sick' joke). We know from various sources that the case referred to, involving a young woman called Mary Channing who had been found guilty of murdering her husband, was one that fascinated and horrified Hardy throughout his life.

To sum up, there is something decidedly unstable about the narrative voice: it makes no attempt at consistency of tone, but moves freely between objectivity and strong personal feelings, and between factual description and the evocation of atmosphere. The historical vision is panoramic, ranging from the Romans to the eighteenth century and the present day, but it is a very personal kind of history, imaginatively recreated in human terms rather than relying on documentation or excavation. This emphasis upon the human, and the continuity of human experience (a favourite Hardyan theme), leads naturally into the mention of Henchard, which in turn links this set-piece with the main narrative of the novel. A scene that has witnessed so many tragedies and so much suffering has a certain appropriateness as a meeting-place for the Mayor and 'his long-lost wife', whom he has treated so badly. An amphitheatre of this kind has been, among other things, virtually a place of human sacrifice, and the opening scene of the novel has recounted the way in which Henchard sacrificed his wife to indulge his own selfish desires.

The reader of the passage is assumed to have an interest in historical matters and also to possess a considerable amount of literary and historical information – of 'general culture', that is, as the period might have understood this concept, and as Hardy's own schooling and self-education had exemplified it. Such allusions as those to 'the spittoon of the Jötuns' (the latter are giants in Norse mythology) and 'Aeolian modulations' (an Aeolian harp produced sounds by the action of the wind) imply a readership with some substantial educational background – in short, a bourgeois and to a large extent urban readership. Similarly, the mention of 'the ruined Coliseum' suggests that readers are likely to have visited Rome, or at least to be well acquainted with its ancient monuments through illustrated books and journals. All of this tells us something about the typical reader of the magazine in which this novel appeared for the first time, and the record of Hardy's career as a novelist shows him both taking advantage of such an audience and hampered by the limitations of its taste and tolerance.

Another point, of a more general nature, is worth making here, since it is one it will be necessary to return to in the discussion of various passages. One aspect of Hardy's powerful visual imagination is a preoccupation with both linear and circular shapes and movements, and with the relationship between the two. His broadly chronological narratives move forward, and his characters are often shown as moving in space as well as time; but there is also a strong element of circularity whereby stories and human destinies tend to return relentlessly to an earlier stage, individual lives moving in circles and the lives of successive generations repeating the experience of their forebears. Michael Henchard's life will turn out to be precisely one such, and the Ring suggests symbolically that despite all his strenuous efforts to move forward and to put the past behind him, that past will persist and his experience will turn out to be circular rather than linear, a regression rather than a progression. As we shall see later, there are other instances of such a symbol in other texts (the young Jude, for example, looks down a circular well as if looking into the future, but finds himself condemned to uncongenial labour in a bowl-shaped field). At the same time there are numerous scenes in which characters travel along a road as if moving purposefully towards a brighter future – a movement that often turns out to be illusory.

Jude the Obscure: Dramatic Method

The next passage to be considered, taken from Hardy's last novel, *Jude the Obscure*, works in a way that is so entirely different from the previous one that the contrast will at once be obvious:

> On the platform stood Arabella. She looked him up and down.
> 'You've been to see her?' she asked.
> 'I have,' said Jude, literally tottering with cold and lassitude.
> 'Well, now you'd best march along home.'
> The water ran out of him as he went, and he was compelled to lean against the wall to support himself while coughing.
> 'You've done for yourself by this, young man,' said she. 'I don't know whether you know it.'
> 'Of course I do. I meant to do for myself.'
> 'What – to commit suicide?'
> 'Certainly.'
> 'Well, I'm blest! Kill yourself for a woman.'
> 'Listen to me, Arabella. You think you are the stronger; and so you are, in a physical sense, now. You could push me over like a ninepin. You did not send that letter the other day, and I could not resent your conduct. But I am not so weak in another way as you think. I made up my mind that a man confined to his room by inflammation of the lungs, a fellow who had only two wishes left in the world, to see a particular woman, and then to die, could neatly accomplish those two wishes at one stroke by taking this journey in the rain. That I've done. I have seen her for the last time, and I've finished myself – put an end to a feverish life which ought never to have been begun!'
> 'Lord – you do talk lofty! Won't you have something warm to drink?'
> 'No thank you. Let's get home.'

They went along by the silent colleges, and Jude kept stopping.

'What are you looking at?'

'Stupid fancies. I see, in a way, those spirits of the dead again, on this my last walk, that I saw when I first walked here!'

'What a curious chap you are!'

'I seem to see them, and almost hear them rustling. But I don't revere all of them as I did then. I don't believe in half of them. The theologians, the apologists, and their kin the metaphysicians, the high-handed statesmen, and others, no longer interest me. All that has been spoilt for me by the grind of stern reality!'

The expression of Jude's corpse-like face in the watery lamplight was indeed as if he saw people where there was nobody. At moments he stood still by an archway, like one watching a figure walk out; then he would look at a window like one discerning a familiar face behind it. He seemed to hear voices, whose words he repeated as if to gather their meaning.

'They seem laughing at me!'

'Who?'

'O – I was talking to myself! The phantoms all about here, in the college archways, and windows. They used to look friendly in the old days, particularly Addison, and Gibbon, and Johnson, and Dr Browne, and Bishop Ken –'

'Come along do! Phantoms! There's neither living nor dead here-abouts except a damn policeman! I never saw the streets emptier.'

'Fancy! The Poet of Liberty used to walk here, and the great Dissector of Melancholy there!'

'I don't want to hear about 'em! They bore me.'

'Walter Raleigh is beckoning to me from that lane – Wycliffe – Harvey – Hooker – Arnold – and a whole crowd of Tractarian Shades –'

'I *don't want* to know their names, I tell you! What do I care about folk dead and gone? Upon my soul you are more sober when you've been drinking than when you have not!'

'I must rest a moment,' he said; and as he paused, holding to the railings, he measured with his eye the height of a college front. 'This is old Rubric. And that Sarcophagus; and up that lane Crozier and Tudor: and all down there is Cardinal with its long front, and its windows with lifted eyebrows, representing the polite surprise of the University at the efforts of such as I.'

'Come along, and I'll treat you!'

'Very well. It will help me home, for I feel the chilly fog from the meadows of Cardinal as if death-claws were grabbing me through and through. As Antigone said, I am neither a dweller among men nor ghosts. But, Arabella, when I am dead, you'll see my spirit flitting up and down here among these!'

'Pooh! You mayn't die after all. You are tough enough yet, old man.'

(Part VI, Chapter 9)

This passage occurs very late in the novel, just after Jude's final journey to Marygreen, where he has seen Sue for the last time and found her still convinced that their relationship has been a sin. He is now back with Arabella, with whom his experience of love and sex began very early in the novel, and it is significant that Jude's life has, near its end, come back to this point. Most novels dealing with growth and education show the protagonist moving forward to encounter new phases of experience, but Hardy's vision, in this final phase of his novel-writing career, is incorrigibly tragic, and there is a sad circularity about Jude's life-pattern. Somewhat similarly, his dreams of success as a scholar have come to nothing, and though he is once again back in Christminster (modelled on Oxford), it is not as a don or a bishop but as a working man without money and too sick to find employment. (A similar circularity may be found in *The Mayor of Casterbridge*, where Henchard near the end of the story is in a very similar situation to where he stood at the beginning; the difference between the two novels is, however, that Henchard's life has shown a 'rise and fall' pattern, whereas Jude, for all his heroic struggles, has never had the chance to rise.)

Technically, the most striking aspect of this passage is the way in which the narrative is conducted very largely through dialogue: the passage could be converted, with very few changes, into a script for radio, television or film, and this reminds us that from a very early stage Hardy's fiction lent itself readily to adaptation for dramatic media. There were numerous stage versions (some by Hardy himself), silent film versions, and later sound film and television versions of many of his novels and stories; very recently, a film titled *Jude* (1996, directed by Michael Winterbottom) and based on this novel has had a considerable success. Hardy had always had a good ear for speech, especially that of the poorer classes: the dialogue of his middle-class characters can sometimes be stilted and unconvincing, but the reviewers of his early works were quick to recognize and applaud his skill in catching the natural tones of uneducated characters – though some suggested, not altogether fairly, that his rustic dialogue owed more to the example of Shakespeare's clowns than to actual 'peasant speech'.

There is certainly little pursuit of charm or picturesqueness, Shakespearean or otherwise, in the dialogue of *Jude the Obscure*. In keeping with the uncompromisingly realistic nature of the novel as a whole, the dialogue has for the most part the authentic flavour of spontaneous speech. Yet there is no question here of 'peasant speech': though Jude's story starts in a village community, most of the action of the novel has taken place in towns and cities, and the lifestyles of both Jude and Arabella have taken on an urban quality. (The reference to the railway station in the opening words of the extract strikes an appropriately modern note, and this is in fact a novel in which the railway plays a significant role.)

Jude, moreover, though an artisan, has acquired a good deal of education, largely self-taught: his socio-economic role is very much at odds with his mental attainments, and he is summed up in a memorable description by an anonymous but perceptive early reviewer (*Saturday Review*, 8 February 1896), who declared, 'That is the voice of the educated proletarian, speaking more distinctly than it has ever spoken before in English literature.' In the passage now under discussion, there is a clear differentiation between the speech of Jude and that of Arabella. Near the beginning her homely phrase 'done for yourself' is echoed, somewhat ironically, by Jude, but his natural tendency is towards a more formal and bookish diction.

In, for instance, the long speech beginning 'Listen to me...' he uses phrases such as 'in a physical sense' and 'a feverish life', and words such as 'accomplish' and 'inflammation', which would not easily be found in Arabella's language. No wonder her reaction to this speech is an ironical one: 'Lord – you do talk lofty!' This 'lofty' talk reflects, of course, Jude's reading, which has concentrated on classical literature, history and theology (very much like Hardy's own youthful studies); Arabella's instincts, on the other hand, are strictly practical and materialistic.

Thus her response to his long and passionate speech is not argument but the offer of 'something warm to drink'. Similarly, his moving reference to the 'spirits of the dead' whom he now sees again on his 'last walk' – for he knows he is dying – prompts only the indifferent response, 'What a curious chap you are!' Thus the difference between the two is not merely one of educational background and tastes but of fundamental outlook and values. That Jude should 'Kill yourself for a woman' is a matter of genuine astonishment to Arabella, who would never dream of killing herself for anyone: her own record, as one of the four major characters in the story, has shown her opportunistically attaching herself to anyone who would serve her purpose for just as long as there was an advantage to be gained by doing so. In a word, while Jude is an idealist, Arabella is a materialist and a pragmatist. Such comments must, however, be regarded as descriptive rather than judgemental: given the severely disadvantaged role of a woman of her class and background in this period, Arabella can hardly be blamed for fighting for survival in the only way open to her, by securing a husband, or at any rate a man, who will serve as a breadwinner. (This point is made clear when she leaves Jude's body in order to go off with the dishonest but persuasive and able-bodied Physician Vilbert.)

The second part of the passage, in which Jude entertains the fancy, and almost the illusion, of seeing the ghosts of distinguished Oxford men, consists less of speech than of soliloquy on Jude's part; he now seems to be thinking aloud – and actually says at one point, 'O – I was talking to myself!' – rather than addressing Arabella, and, sensing this, she shows irritation at his disregard of her. To Arabella, the names of the famous dead mean nothing, but she perceives them as rivals for Jude's attention. Again, her bluntly expressed pragmatic attitude is shown in her dismissal in a single phrase of all the traditions that mean so much to Jude: 'What do I care about folk dead and gone?' Finally, Jude's eloquent recitation of the names of Oxford colleges (fictional here, but corresponding to recognizable originals), his vivid description of his physical state ('as if death-claws were grabbing me through and through'), and his despairing quotation from Sophocles's *Antigone*, stand in effective contrast to Arabella's rough and casual words of comfort.

Unlike the excerpt from *The Mayor of Casterbridge* discussed earlier in this chapter, the narrator's role in this passage is a subordinate one, the fictional business being largely conducted through speech, and such concomitants of speech as bodily movement and facial expression. We are therefore justified in describing the method as dramatic rather than analytic: the reader learns about the feelings of Jude and Arabella and the relationship between them not by being *told* about these matters in an objective, summarizing manner but by *listening* to the two of them talking and by *observing* their behaviour. Two issues help to charge the realistic dialogue with intensity: our awareness that Jude, despite Arabella's rough comfort, is close to death, and the question of how, given the gulf existing between them in spite of their patched-up relationship, she will react to the sickness and death that await him. The last few pages of the novel provide the answer to this question.

Tess of the d'Urbervilles: the Narrative of Indirection

The climax of the story in *Tess of the d'Urbervilles* involves violent action, the murder of Alec by Tess, and, as we shall see, this presents the novelist with a problem. In the following passage, a scene involving two major characters, Tess and Alec, is mediated through the consciousness of a minor character, the landlady in whose lodgings the couple are staying. When the passage opens, the landlady, who is curious about the behaviour of her guests and has been peering through the keyhole in her anxiety to find out what is going on, is listening at the door:

> There were more and sharper words from the man; then a sudden rustle; and she had sprung to her feet. Mrs Brooks, thinking that the speaker was coming to rush out of the door, hastily retreated down the stairs.
>
> She need not have done so, however, for the door of the sitting-room was not opened. But Mrs Brooks felt it unsafe to watch on the landing again, and entered her own parlour below.

She could hear nothing through the floor, although she listened intently, and thereupon went to the kitchen to finish her interrupted breakfast. Coming up presently to the front room on the ground floor she took up some sewing, waiting for her lodgers to ring that she might take away the breakfast, which she meant to do herself, to discover what was the matter if possible. Overhead, as she sat, she could now hear the floorboards slightly creak, as if some one were walking about, and presently the movement was explained by the rustle of garments against the banisters, the opening and the closing of the front door, and the form of Tess passing to the gate on her way into the street. She was fully dressed now in the walking costume of a well-to-do young lady in which she had arrived, with the sole addition that over her hat and black feathers a veil was drawn.

Mrs Brooks had not been able to catch any word of farewell, temporary or otherwise, between her tenants at the door above. They might have quarrelled, or Mr d'Urberville might still be asleep, for he was not an early riser.

She went into the back room which was more especially her own apartment, and continued her sewing there. The lady lodger did not return, nor did the gentleman ring his bell. Mrs Brooks pondered on the delay, and on what probable relation the visitor who had called so early bore to the couple upstairs. In reflecting she leant back in her chair.

As she did so her eyes glanced casually over the ceiling till they were arrested by a spot in the middle of its white surface which she had never noticed there before. It was about the size of a wafer when she first observed it, but it speedily grew as large as the palm of her hand, and then she could perceive that it was red. The oblong white ceiling, with this scarlet blot in the midst, had the appearance of a gigantic ace of hearts.

Mrs Brooks had strange qualms of misgiving. She got upon the table, and touched the spot in the ceiling with her fingers. It was damp, and she fancied that it was a blood stain.

Descending from the table, she left the parlour, and went upstairs, intending to enter the room overhead, which was the bedchamber at the back of the drawing-room. But, nerveless woman as she had now become, she could not bring herself to attempt the handle. She listened. The dead silence within was broken only by a regular beat.

Drip, drip, drip.

Mrs Brooks hastened downstairs, opened the front door, and ran
into the street.

(Chapter 56)

In writing this scene Hardy faced, and solved, an interesting
narrative problem. The episode, economically recounted, arguably
forms the climax of the whole novel: from Tess's first meeting with
Alec near the beginning, everything that has happened between them
has led to this *dénouement*, in which Tess avenges herself on the man
who has exploited and seduced her and who, at least indirectly, has
destroyed her marriage to Angel Clare. The heroine, who has
throughout been a figure who suffers rather than initiating events,
now resorts to an uncharacteristic moment of action – indeed, of
violence – as she snatches up the nearest weapon to hand and stabs
Alec to the heart. The novelist's problem is to render the scene
dramatic without sacrificing the reader's sympathy for Tess, and he
must have been aware that to have shown this gentle and good-
hearted girl committing violent and bloody murder might have upset
or offended many of his readers.

In arriving at his brilliantly simple solution to this problem, Hardy
may well have been influenced by the conventions of a literary genre
very remote from the Victorian novel: the tragic drama of classical
Greece. As a young man he had carefully studied these in the original
Greek, and was very familiar with the convention whereby tragic
events in such dramas are not shown onstage but are normally
recounted by a messenger. In Sophocles's *King Oedipus*, the self-
blinding of the hero and the suicide of his wife–mother Jocasta
take place offstage. In this extract from *Tess*, Hardy filters the lurid
and violent events through the commonplace mind of a very minor
character who is observed with irony. Mrs Brooks, the landlady of
the seaside lodgings where Tess and Alec are staying, undergoes a
series of emotions that range from mild curiosity to horror and panic,
and in this way the ghastly events that take place in the room that the
reader never enters are communicated.

Hardy's locations are rarely mere 'background' but are significant
in relation to character and event, and The Herons, Sandbourne, is
no exception. This is a house that, in the course of the passage, we

get to know well: the disposition of the rooms is so clearly indicated that we could draw a plan of it. Architecturally, as Hardy the ex-architect would have been well aware, it is as commonplace as its owner, and identical with others in the street: a product, that is, of modern capitalist enterprise rather than one built of local materials for a family who will live in it for generations (as Hardy's own family had done in the Bockhampton cottage, now owned by the National Trust).

Unlike most of Hardy's settings, the fashionable seaside town of Sandbourne (based on Bournemouth) is an urban rather than a rural environment; to this extent it is consistent with the depiction of Alec as a rootless figure and also one who is worldly and ostentatious as well as free with his money – more precisely, with his father's money, since Alec seems never to have done a day's work in his life. Here Tess finds herself in profoundly unnatural surroundings, as she was not (for instance) during Angel's courtship of her at Talbothays farm: the role of a rich man's mistress, which she has adopted in despair and desperation, is not one that comes easily to her. Hardy makes the point with a simple but telling visual detail: always interested in female dress, he refers to Tess's leaving the house 'in the walking costume of a well-to-do young lady' – a garb in which we may find it difficult to recognize the Tess of earlier scenes in the novel.

But the most striking feature of the whole passage is the negative one that we have no access to Tess's mind throughout this scene: her emotions as she is driven to extremes can only be conjectured. (For comments by a leading Hardy critic on the 'avoidance of analysis' in the presentation of Tess as a whole, see p. 185 below.) Instead we have voices heard through a door, the creaking of floorboards heard through the celing, the 'rustle' of a woman's long and full-skirted dress as she comes downstairs, the opening and closing of the front door, and a figure glimpsed for a moment as it moves quickly away. These are the details of the scene; the central event, the sudden snatching up of the knife and its plunge into Alec's chest, is a gap or silence. To recount this explicitly would have been too painful, too horrifying; and even as it is, Hardy seems to try to counteract the horror through a kind of neutralizing, sanitizing or distancing irony. Consider, for example, the semi-ludicrous pictures of the respectable landlady first listening at the keyhole of her guests' room, then beating a hasty retreat downstairs when she thinks they are about to emerge, and finally – and more grimly, though still semi-comically – standing on the table to touch the spot that has appeared on her hitherto immaculate ceiling.

That scarlet spot is a brilliant narrative stroke, simultaneously realistic and symbolic. It announces, silently but irresistibly, the deed that has led to the death of Alec, and the way in which it transforms the plain white ceiling into a kind of gigantic ace of hearts suggests that human fate (including that of Tess) is subject to the blind laws of chance no less than a game of cards. At the same time it forms part of a pattern of allusions to the colour red that runs throughout the novel, ranging from the red sash worn by Tess over her white dress when the reader first meets her to the life-blood of the horse Prince spilt on the road. It is entirely characteristic of Hardy's narrative technique to highlight a moment of drama with a striking visual image, but in this instance the unusual feature is the mediation of the incident through a character who stands, so to speak, on the extreme periphery of the action. Another novelist might have shown us Tess delivering the blow and Alec's blood forming a pool on the floor (Joseph Conrad does something very similar in his description in *The Secret Agent* (1907) of Winnie Verloc's murder of her husband by stabbing him through the heart with a carving-knife); but Hardy's method both creates suspense and distances Tess, who in the remaining portion of the novel withdraws more and more from the scene of action.

The prose of this passage reflects the shift from the banal situation of the opening – the inquisitive landlady eavesdropping on her guests – to the mounting mystery of just what is going on in the upstairs room (to which the reader, like the landlady, is denied access), and to the suspicion and then horror as she (and the reader) becomes aware of what has happened. The prose of the opening lines is plain, even flat, in its absence of colour and emphasis, but soon suggestion and irony begin to intrude. The 'black feathers' of Tess's fashionable hat might well have reminded a Victorian reader of the black ostrich plumes used to decorate the horses pulling a hearse, while the land-lady's idea that Alec might still be asleep is unconsciously ironic – he will never wake again. Even the cliche 'dead silence' takes on, in this context, a sinister meaning. This progression from the commonplace to the horrific – from the comic opening image of the landlady springing to her feet in alarm to the melodramatic 'Drip, drip, drip' – is reflected in the changing moods and emotions of Mrs Brooks, who thus acts as a kind of representative of the reader within the action of this scene.

In this passage, then, we gain no insight into Tess's state of mind in the moments that lead up to the murder: the method is dramatic rather than psychological. Indeed, we learn much more about the landlady's feelings than about the heroine's. In a similar way, Hardy denies us access to Tess's consciousness in the final phase of the story, after her arrest: whereas some novelists (Dickens, for example) might have made much of her trial and her time in the condemned cell, these are not described by Hardy, and we do not even see her on the scaffold, since her death is simply though effectively announced by yet another visual image, the hoisting of a black flag over the jail.

Far from the Madding Crowd and Psychological Analysis

In the final extract to be considered in this chapter, taken from *Far from the Madding Crowd*, the technique is very different and we are given the kind of analysis of the heroine's state of mind that Hardy partly learned from George Eliot (interestingly enough, some reviewers of the anonymously published serial version of *Far from the Madding Crowd* speculated that Eliot might be the author). In this passage Bathsheba confronts the coffin of Fanny Robin, who has been seduced by Sergeant Troy and, after great suffering, has died bearing his child. Already suspicious of her husband's relationship with Fanny, she is in an agony of suspense and uncertainty, and cannot rest until she knows the truth, one way or the other, about the circumstances of Fanny's death:

> More fevered now by a reaction from the first feelings which Oak's example had raised in her, she paused in the hall, looking at the door of the room wherein Fanny lay. She locked her fingers, threw back her

head, and strained her hot hands rigidly across her forehead, saying, with a hysterical sob, 'Would to God you would speak and tell me your secret, Fanny!...O, I hope, hope it is not true that there are two of you!...If I could only look in upon you for one little minute, I should know all!'

A few moments passed, and she added, slowly, '*And I will.*'

Bathsheba in after times could never gauge the mood which carried her through the actions following this murmured resolution on this memorable evening of her life. She went to the lumber-closet for a screw-driver. At the end of a short though undefined time she found herself in the small room, quivering with emotion, a mist before her eyes, and an excruciating pulsation in her brain, standing beside the uncovered coffin of the girl whose conjectured end had so entirely engrossed her, and saying to herself in a husky voice as she gazed within –

'It was best to know the worst, and I know it now!'

She was conscious of having brought about this situation by a series of actions done as by one in an extravagant dream; of following that idea as to method, which had burst upon her in the hall with glaring obviousness, by gliding to the top of the stairs, assuring herself by listening to the heavy breathing of her maids that they were asleep, gliding down again, turning the handle of the door within which the young girl lay, and deliberately setting herself to do what, if she had anticipated any such undertaking at night and alone, would have horrified her, but which, when done, was not so dreadful as was the conclusive proof of her husband's conduct which came with knowing beyond doubt the last chapter of Fanny's story.

Bathsheba's head sank upon her bosom, and the breath which had been bated in suspense, curiosity, and interest, was exhaled now in the form of a whispered wail: 'Oh-h-h!' she said, and the silent room added length to her moan.

Her tears fell fast beside the unconscious pair in the coffin: tears of a complicated origin, of a nature indescribable, almost indefinable except as other than those of simple sorrow. Assuredly their wonted fires must have lived in Fanny's ashes when events were so shaped as to chariot her hither in this natural, unobtrusive, yet effectual manner. The one feat alone – that of dying – by which a mean condition could be resolved into a grand one, Fanny had achieved. And to that had destiny subjoined this encounter tonight, which had, in Bathsheba's wild imagining, turned her companion's failure to success, her humiliation to triumph, her lucklessness to ascendancy; it had thrown over herself a garish light of mockery, and set upon all things about her an ironical smile.

Fanny's face was framed in by that yellow hair of hers; and there was no longer much room for doubt as to the origin of the curl owned by Troy. In Bathsheba's heated fancy the innocent white countenance expressed a dim triumphant consciousness of the pain she was retaliating for her pain with all the merciless rigour of the Mosaic law: 'Burning for burning; wound for wound; strife for strife.'

(Chapter 43)

Reading this passage, we have a strong sense of the narrator's presence throughout: Bathsheba is alone, and apart from a few exclamations that are forced from her by her emotions, it is the narrator's 'voice' that monopolizes our attention. At the same time, as already suggested earlier in this chapter, the Hardyan narrator cannot usually be characterized as 'omniscient' in the traditional sense, and here there are some clear indications of the limits of narrative consciousness and authority – an awareness that certain things remain permanently unknowable. Bathsheba enters the room 'At the end of a short though undefined time', and of course the time could easily have been more specifically indicated through some such phrase as 'after a minute or two'; Hardy gives us, however, a temporary merging of the narrator's consciousness with that of the character, since the inability to be sure how long had passed is Bathsheba's. The phrase is thus a natural development of the suggestion two sentences earlier that 'Bathsheba in after times could never gauge the mood...'. Hardy wants us to understand that at certain crises of life we may act in a way that is unconsciously motivated and not within the control of our reason and understanding, and that the sources of such actions are incapable of being fully understood. Clearly such psychological insights cannot be accommodated within a tradition of narratorial omniscience.

Other parts of the passage reinforce this sense of Bathsheba driven to an extraordinary and appalling act by feelings beyond her control or understanding – including the narrator's understanding;

and, by implication, the reader's. She is compared to 'one in an extravagant dream'. Later, when she weeps over the occupants of the open coffin, her emotions are described as 'of a complicated origin, of a nature indescribable, almost indefinable...'. This rendering of a complex emotional state, elusive of definition, is, however, balanced by a strong sense of physicality. Among male novelists Hardy is outstanding for his insights into the lives and emotions of women, and here the solitary heroine expresses her state of mind partly through body language. Trying to summon up courage to enter the room, 'She locked her fingers, threw back her head, and strained her hot hands rigidly across her forehead,' actions that demonstrate the physical tension that is a counterpart of her mental state. Later, having discovered what the coffin contains, she is described as 'quivering with emotion, a mist before her eyes, and an excruciating pulsation in her brain'. Indications of the way in which she speaks ('a hysterical sob', 'in a husky voice') also convey a sense of Bathsheba's physicality. Hardy wants his readers to have a vivid and painful insight into Bathsheba's state of mind, but he also wants to give us a strong awareness of her physical presence, of what it is like to inhabit a woman's body at such a moment of exceptional emotion and sensation.

Apart from its intrinsic power and local effectiveness, the passage forms a turning-point in the action of the novel. Bathsheba's marriage to Troy has inevitably had a profound effect on her relationship with the novel's hero, Gabriel Oak, the vicissitudes of which have dominated the early stages of the story. But her discovery of Troy's relationship with Fanny in turn affects her marriage and lays the ground for the disappearance, presumed death, reappearance and actual death of Troy, which constitute a large part of the drama of the closing phases. As so often, Hardy makes use of a trivial object for far-reaching and almost symbolic purposes: the lock of hair that Bathsheba had earlier noticed in Troy's possession is now conclusively identified in her mind as belonging to Fanny, and offers painful evidence of her husband's attachment to the other woman.

In considering the previous extract examined in this chapter, we noted how Tess's murder of Alec takes place outside the text – a narrative silence dictated by the wish to spare the reader feelings of pain or horror, and also the need to avoid showing the heroine at a moment of uncharacteristic passion and violence. On a smaller scale there is something similar here: after Bathsheba's shocking decision to satisfy her unbearable curiosity by opening the coffin, there is a vague reference to 'the actions following this murmured resolution', but there follows a gap in the narrative between her fetching the screw-driver and, a few words later, her standing beside 'the uncovered coffin'. As with Tess, Hardy seems disinclined to show his heroine engaged in violent action.

For somewhat different reasons, there is considerable narrative tact with regard to the stillborn baby that lies in the arms of its dead mother: the veiled expressions conveying Bathsheba's recognition that she now 'knows the worst' and knows 'beyond doubt the last chapter of Fanny's story', and the much more explicit but still discreet reference to 'the unconscious pair in the coffin', show an awareness on Hardy's part that he would not be permitted by his editor and publishers to say anything that might offend the readers of the magazine in which the novel first appeared.

The editor of the *Cornhill Magazine*, Leslie Stephen, in fact wrote to Hardy specifically on this point: 'May I suggest that Troy's seduction of the young woman will require to be treated in a gingerly fashion, when, as I suppose must be the case, he comes to be exposed to his wife? I mean that the thing must be stated but that the words must be careful – excuse this wretched shred of concession to public stupidity; but I am a slave' (Stephen's letter is quoted in R. L. Purdy, *Thomas Hardy: A Bibliographical Study* (Oxford, 1954), pp. 338–9). At a stage in his career when he was still trying to establish himself as a novelist, Hardy seems to have been quite willing to obey the injunction that 'the words must be careful'. But Stephen was an established man of letters, and it is evidence of the power of the reader, and the extent to which commercial considerations were influential, that he too should have been prepared to make concessions to 'public stupidity'.

As one would expect in a passage largely concerned with analysing feelings and states of mind, the language contains many abstractions. Phrases like 'suspense, curiosity, and interest' seek to define Bathsheba's mental state by recourse to abstract nouns, and such expressions as 'conclusive proof', 'nature indescribable' and 'merciless rigour' also belong to the discourse of intellectual and psychological analysis. But there are also varieties of diction that contrast with these, such as the homely reference (grim enough in its context, though) to a 'screw-driver', and the simple but vivid image of the dead woman, her face 'framed in by that yellow hair of hers'.

Particularly notable from a stylistic point of view is the paragraph beginning 'She was conscious...', which consists of a single very long sentence. This disregards, for calculated dramatic effect, the normal conventions of syntax, piling phrase on phrase and clause on clause in a verbal re-enactment of Bathsheba's behaviour. Just as, in her excitement and distress, Hardy's heroine moves rapidly from one action to the next, the sentence presses relentlessly forward without giving the reader a resting-place. The effect is deliberately breathless, miming the breathlessness of the character. For some of the original readers, indeed, the sentence would literally have produced breathlessness, since reading instalments of fiction aloud in the family circle was a well-established Victorian custom (and a further reason for sensitivity where questions of propriety were concerned).

A final point concerns two allusions in the passage, one submerged, the other on the surface. At the end there is a direct quotation from the Old Testament: 'Mosaic law' is the law of Moses, particularly as enshrined in the Ten Commandments, and the quotation (not quite accurate, suggesting that Hardy was quoting from memory) comes from the Book of Exodus. Earlier, in the paragraph beginning 'Her tears fell fast...', there is a much less obvious allusion to a very famous eighteenth-century poem, Thomas Gray's 'Elegy Written in a Country Churchyard', and the allusion is so skilfully worked into Hardy's own sentence that the editor of at least one paperback edition of the novel has not spotted it. In an age of aristocratic privilege, Gray insists that the poor, including the rural poor, share a common humanity and capacity for feeling with the wealthy and powerful; this theme, which no doubt helped to account for the poem's immense popularity, would certainly have commended it to Hardy, who took the title of his novel from line 73 of Gray's poem ('Far from the madding crowd's ignoble strife'); for comments on the irony of this title, see p. 164 below.

A few lines later (89–92), referring to the deathbeds of the humble, Gray writes:

> On some fond breast the parting soul relies,
> Some pious drops the closing eye requires;
> Ev'n from the tomb the voice of nature cries,
> Ev'n in our ashes live their wonted fires.

As with the Biblical quotation, Hardy assumes a widely shared literary culture and a readership likely to be intimately familiar with this celebrated poem, and adapts the last line of this stanza to his own purpose: 'their wonted fires must have lived in Fanny's ashes'. His intention must also have been to invoke the reader's recollections of the lines that precede this one, which take on a sad irony in relation to Fanny: she has died alone and in misery, with no 'fond breast' or 'pious drops' to offer comfort.

Both of these quotations give the death of this obscure young woman an added solemnity by associating it with ancient and widely familiar texts that express aspects of the universal experience of mankind. The thrust of the last two paragraphs of the passage is that Fanny in death has achieved a dignity, and even a superiority to the living Bathsheba, that she never had in life. This is not, however, mere philosophizing or sentimentality, for the psychological point that is implicit is that Bathsheba now sees Fanny as a serious rival for Troy's love. The 'triumphant consciousness' that Bathsheba seems to detect on the face of the corpse is in fact a projection of her own anxieties, and events are to prove her justified, since Troy's penitence for being the indirect cause of Fanny's death causes a rupture between him and his wife. In this way, again, the passage is not only immediately effective but looks forward to later developments in the story.

Conclusions

In this chapter we have seen that a novel by Hardy (and the same is true of much other fiction) can contain components of very different kinds. The passage from *The Mayor of Casterbridge* showed the narrator assuming the role of essayist or historian in describing an archaeological site; at the same time it was possible to note a certain instability of tone as the narrator's (and perhaps also the author's) personal attitudes infiltrated the apparently impersonal and objective commentary. In complete contrast, the scene from *Jude the Obscure* is dramatic in form, conveying information to the reader largely through the realistic dialogue intended to represent the spontaneous speech of two characters.

In the murder scene from *Tess of the d'Urbervilles*, dramatic method is also used, but with an important difference. For here the emphasis is on action rather than speech, and the central events are not presented directly but mediated through a minor character, who listens, observes and deduces. Finally, in the excerpt from *Far from the Madding Crowd*, though there is action of a startling kind when Bathsheba opens the coffin, the main concern is with internal rather than external happenings – that is, with the psychological analysis of Bathsheba's thoughts and emotions.

Methods of Analysis

In the examination of these four passages, special attention has been paid to the idea of 'voices' in the novel. Each of the major characters is endowed with a distinctive mode of speech, so that, for example, Gabriel Oak's speeches could not be mistaken for those of Sergeant Troy, or Arabella's for Sue's. This creation of an 'idiolect' or individual mode of speech is done in various ways that include characteristic types of vocabulary or syntax (sentence-patterns), as well as such features as dialect and non-standard pronunciations. Thus, Oak's vocabulary is that of the countryman while Troy's reflects his military life; Sue's sentences tend to be longer than those used by Arabella, and she favours a more abstract, intellectual, even academic vocabulary.

In addition to this large chorus of individual voices, often set in contrast to one another (as in the scene from *Jude* quoted above), the narrator also – and perhaps most importantly – has a voice, or several voices. The language used by Hardy's narrators can be straightforward or ironic, simple or learned, objective or rhetorical. The narrator can also perform a variety of functions – narrating action, describing characters or scenes, commenting and generalizing. Analysis of a passage will often involve paying attention to these different functions and to the 'voices' through which they are transmitted to the reader. We can also ask the question: What kind of reader is implied by the use of a particular 'voice'? Describing the *characters* of a novel is a familiar enough operation, but we ought also to be able to characterize the *narrator* and the 'ideal' or imagined *reader*.

Suggestions for Further Work

For another example of a passage in which the narrator monopolizes the reader's attention, you may like to consider the second chapter of *Far from the Madding Crowd*, from the beginning to '... the altitudes of the stars'.

Another good example of narratorial intervention will be found in the account of Alec's seduction of Tess in Chapter 11 of *Tess of the d'Urbervilles*: see especially the last three paragraphs of that chapter for a direct appeal to the reader to become involved in the question of responsibility for Tess's fate.

For a contrasting example of dramatic method, see *The Mayor of Casterbridge*, Chapter 3, from 'Reaching the outskirts of the village...' to the end of the chapter. Another example of great power and interest is the pig-killing scene in *Jude the Obscure* (Part I, Chapter 10, from the beginning to '... bitterness in his amusement').

2

Beginnings and Endings

Introduction

Since the nature of language is linear, one word following another, literary texts must inescapably have beginnings and endings. In an obvious sense, however, no story (as opposed to narrative) ever really begins or ends: it is always possible to think of something that happened before the beginning and something that may happen after the end. As a result the decisions that novelists make as to where to start and conclude their narratives are often of considerable interest, and Hardy's solutions to these problems are worth careful examination.

Many modern writers have sought to play down what they have perceived as the artificiality of beginnings and endings, and to convey the impression that the narrative they present is only part of a continuous, unbroken flow of experience and consciousness. Virginia Woolf's *Mrs Dalloway* (1925) begins quite abruptly with the statement that 'Mrs Dalloway said she would buy the flowers herself'; Ernest Hemingway's *A Moveable Feast* (1964) begins 'Then there was the bad weather', the first word of this sentence plainly implying that something has preceded it – some ghostly text antecedent to the printed text and containing a narrative prior to that with which the printed text is concerned. Nineteenth-century writers, in contrast, often make no attempt to pretend that the beginning is anything but a beginning: the first sentence of Dickens's *David Copperfield* (1850) draws attention to the storyteller and the act of storytelling that has just been embarked on, and the common-est kind of opening carefully locates the impending narrative in time and place, often quite precisely. Occasional exceptions to this rule, like the intense and 'modern' opening of Charlotte Brontë's *Jane Eyre* (1847), are striking by reason of their comparative rarity.

When it comes to conclusions, the nineteenth-century tradition generally favours the kind of apparent finality represented by such events as deaths and weddings (though a wedding is a good example of the kind of ending that is, from another point of view, a beginning). Most of Dickens's novels end with the unravelling of secrets and mysteries and the distribution of rewards and punish-ments. George Eliot's *The Mill on the Floss* (1860) ends with the death of the two principal characters, and *Jane Eyre* with the event announced in the narrator's famous words, 'Reader, I married him.' There are, however, some interesting examples of dissidence from this tradition. Another novel by Charlotte Brontë, *Villette* (1853), ends ambiguously, and Dickens wrote two different endings for *Great Expectations* (1861) that embody different degrees of finality.

Hardy's practice characteristically blends conservatism and innova-tion. The demands of publishers, editors and readers pushed him in the direction of traditional kinds of ending, but his instinct was often to subvert this tradition in the interests of moral honesty and psychological realism. In an essay on 'Candour in English Fiction', published in 1890, he refers ironically to 'the false colouring best expressed by the regulation finish that "they married and were happy ever after"', and as early as *Under the Greenwood Tree* (1872), his second published novel, he was already quietly sabotaging that complacent and largely unquestioned tradition. This short pastoral novel ends, like classical comedy, with marriage celebrations and dancing, but the final note is more ambiguous and bitter-sweet. The simple-hearted Dick has asked his bride to promise that they will 'have no secrets from each other', and she, more devious, has cannily responded 'None from today'; the final words of the novel tell us that she 'thought of a secret she would never tell'. The sense of marriage as ensuring a state of stability and security is qualified by these words, which hint at a future beyond the text that will have its own problems and imperfections.

A little later in his career, Hardy opened *The Return of the Native* in a way that is unusual and original in its concentration on the non-human world. The landscape is first presented in terms of geological time rather than human history, and only very gradually is a human element permitted to emerge, first in the form of a road, then as a vehicle, and finally as a human individual. At the very outset Hardy seems to be calling on his readers to think of the drama that will be unfolded – a very limited one in terms of time and space and the number of individuals involved – in a context that is both universal and elemental. As we shall see in a moment, the opening of *The Mayor of Casterbridge* offers a more restricted variation on this concept of an opening in which humanity is dwarfed by being placed in an extensive landscape – and dwarfed, too, in another sense by being seen in relation to a natural environment that represents continuity beyond the scope of individual lives, and also indifference to those lives.

However, when he came to the ending of *The Return of the Native*, Hardy was driven to compromise. A footnote at the end of the penultimate chapter states that 'the original conception of the story' did not involve a marriage between Diggory and Thomasin – a clear concession to the popular taste for happy endings – but that 'certain circumstances of serial publication led to a change of intent'; Hardy adds wryly that readers can 'choose between the endings', while at the same time making it perfectly clear that his own preference is for the more honest, less sentimental ending.

The Mayor of Casterbridge: a Family without a Name

As might be expected in a novel-writing career that extends over a quarter of a century, Hardy's practice with regard to beginnings and endings is not entirely consistent. There are, however, some recurring and distinctive features, and this chapter will seek to elucidate them through an examination of two beginnings and two endings. Here is the opening of *The Mayor of Casterbridge*:

One evening of late summer, before the nineteenth century had reached one-third of its span, a young man and woman, the latter carrying a child, were approaching the large village of Weydon-Priors, in Upper Wessex, on foot. They were plainly but not ill clad, though the thick hoar of dust which had accumulated on their shoes and garments from an obviously long journey lent a disadvantageous shabbiness to their appearance just now.

The man was of fine figure, swarthy, and stern in aspect; and he showed in profile a facial angle so slightly inclined as to be almost perpendicular. He wore a short jacket of brown corduroy, newer than the remainder of his suit, which was a fustian waistcoat with white horn buttons, breeches of the same, tanned leggings, and a straw hat overlaid with black glazed canvas. At his back he carried by a looped strap a rush basket; from which protruded at one end the crutch of a hay-knife, a wimble for hay-bonds being also visible in the aperture. His measured, springless walk was the walk of the skilled countryman as distinct from the desultory shamble of the general labourer; while in the turn and plant of each foot there was, further, a dogged and cynical indifference personal to himself, showing its presence even in the regularly interchanging fustian folds, now in the left leg, now in the right, as he paced along.

What was really peculiar, however, in this couple's progress, and would have attracted the attention of any casual observer otherwise disposed to overlook them, was the perfect silence they preserved. They walked side by side in such a way as to suggest afar off the low, easy, confidential chat of people full of reciprocity; but on closer view it could be discerned that the man was reading, or pre- tending to read, a ballad sheet which he kept before his eyes with some difficulty by the hand that was passed through the basket strap. Whether this apparent cause were the real cause, or whether it were an assumed one to escape an intercourse that would have been irksome to him, nobody but himself could have said precisely; but his taciturnity was unbroken, and the woman enjoyed no society whatever from his presence. Virtually she walked the highway alone, save for the child she bore. Sometimes the man's bent elbow almost touched her shoulder, for she kept as close to his side as was possible without actual contact, but she seemed to have no idea of taking his arm, nor he of offering it; and far from exhibiting surprise at his ignoring silence she appeared to receive it as a natural thing. If any word at all were uttered by the little group, it was an occasional whisper of the woman to the child – a tiny girl in short clothes and blue boots of knitted yarn – and the murmured babble of the child in reply.

The chief – almost the only – attraction of the young woman's face was its mobility. When she looked down sideways to the girl she became pretty, and even handsome, particularly that in the action her features caught slantwise the rays of the strongly coloured sun, which made transparencies of her eyelids and nostrils and set fire on her lips. When she plodded on in the shade of the hedge, silently thinking, she had the hard, half-apathetic expression of one who deems anything possible at the hands of Time and Chance except, perhaps, fair play. The first phase was the work of Nature, the second probably of civilization.

That the man and woman were husband and wife, and the parents of the girl in arms, there could be little doubt. No other than such relationship would have accounted for the atmosphere of stale familiarity which the trio carried along with them like a nimbus as they moved down the road.

The wife mostly kept her eyes fixed ahead, though with little interest – the scene for that matter being one that might have been matched at almost any spot in any county in England at this time of the year; a road neither straight nor crooked, neither level nor hilly, bordered by hedges, trees, and other vegetation, which had entered the blackened-green stage of colour that the doomed leaves pass through on their way to dingy, and yellow, and red. The grassy margin of the bank, and the nearest hedgerow boughs, were powdered by the dust that had been stirred over them by hasty vehicles, the same dust as it lay on the road deadening their footfalls like a carpet; and this, with the aforesaid total absence of conversation, allowed every extraneous sound to be heard.

For a long time there was none, beyond the voice of a weak bird singing a trite old evening song that might doubtless have been heard on the hill at the same hour, and with the self-same trills, quavers, and breves, at any sunset of that season for centuries untold. But as they approached the village sundry distant shouts and rattles reached their ears from some elevated spot in that direction, as yet screened from view by foliage. When the outlying houses of Weydon-Priors could just be described, the family group was met by a turnip-hoer with his hoe on his shoulder, and his dinner-bag suspended from it. The reader promptly glanced up.

'Any trade doing here?' he asked phlegmatically, designating the village in his van by a wave of the broadsheet. And thinking the labourer did not understand him, he added, 'Anything in the hay-trussing line?'

(Chapter 1)

At first glance, the long opening sentence seems characteristic of nineteenth-century realist fiction: earlier novelists such as Scott, Thackeray and George Eliot all favour the kind of opening that firmly places characters in the context of a more or less precisely located time and place, enabling the reader to situate the action in relation to familiar elements of topography and history. Thus, George Eliot (an important influence on Hardy) opens her *Silas Marner* (1861), 'In the days when the spinning-wheels hummed busily in the farmhouses...'; more precisely, she begins *Felix Holt* (1866), 'On the 1st of September, in the memorable year 1832, some one was expected at Transome Court.' It has even been suggested that the opening words of *The Mayor of Casterbridge* echo those of Thackeray's *Vanity Fair* (1848), 'While the present century was in its teens...'. In the Hardyan example there is, however, one slightly unusual feature, in that the individuals are not named but are simply 'a young man', a 'woman' and 'a child'. As it turns out, the reader has to wait quite a long time before discovering the names of Michael, Susan and Elizabeth-Jane Henchard, and this refusal on the narrator's part to grant the characters the individuality that personal names bestow gives them a representative quality. Initially, they are in a sense Everyman, Everywoman and Everychild travelling along a road that is not just a line on the map but a metaphor for life-experience.

Thus, for the time being, these unnamed individuals are any family travelling any road, and Hardy seems closer to allegory than to realistic fiction. There may also perhaps be an allusion – more readily picked up by readers in an age when familiarity with the Bible was commonplace – to the Holy Family and the story of the Flight into Egypt by Joseph, Mary and the infant Jesus. Hardy is a highly allusive writer, and references, explicit or otherwise, to the Bible are probably commoner in his work than those to any other literary source. This possibility finds support later in the passage, in the use of the uncommon word 'nimbus', signifying the kind of halo that was placed around the heads of saints by classical painters. It needs to be added, though, that the hinted similarity to the Holy Family is ironic: in the godless age in which Hardy is acutely conscious of living and writing, this is a family group and a journey that are wearisomely banal ('stale familiarity') rather than historic or mythological.

In accordance with the conventions of realistic fiction, the references to time and place seem reasonably precise: the historical moment in question is a certain time of day, at a certain season of the year, around 1830. Since this is a novel of the 1880s, therefore, the initial action is located more than half a century earlier, before the birth of many of the original readers (as also of the author himself). It would, however, have been a time remembered by older readers, and one that younger readers might have heard of from their parents or grandparents (as, again, Hardy most certainly did). So that while this promises to be in a sense a historical novel rather than one of contemporary life, it also promises to treat of a very accessible kind of history, a history that has palpably helped to make the present what it is. We shall also find before long that the opening pages of the novel constitute a kind of prologue, and that the main action takes place much closer to the mid-century – the period when Hardy himself was growing up.

As for the topographical references, these both are and are not precise. 'Weydon-Priors' and 'Upper Wessex' sound like plausible names for a village and a county, but in fact neither can be found on the map of south-west England. On the other hand they correspond fairly closely to places that *can* be found on the map: the fictional 'Upper Wessex' corresponds quite closely to the county of Hampshire, and in describing 'Weydon-Priors' Hardy had in mind, and partly borrowed the name of, a village called Weyhill. In effect Hardy is preserving his creative freedom by refusing to commit himself to a depiction of actual places, at the same time that he is drawing generously on his own local knowledge. What this amounts to, as with the characters who at this stage both are and are not individuals, is that Hardy's 'realism' is of a distinctly qualified kind: while seeming to conform to well-established patterns of Victorian fiction, he is free to write the kind of story that may have non-realistic elements – may, for example, take on the dimensions of fable, allegory or myth. At such points we need to be mindful that, for all his long commitment to fiction, Hardy was first and last a poet who saw himself as, or at least aspired to be, the heir of the great Romantic poets. (See pp. 169–70 for examples of the readiness with which his prose fiction lent itself to transformation into poems.)

The second part of the opening paragraph is revealing in relation to the role of the narrator. The travellers are 'plainly but not ill clad', and this defining detail places them socially and economically, for they belong to a period when, as any Victorian photograph of a street scene demonstrates, dress was more obviously an index of status than it is today. The plain but adequate clothing shows that they are, despite their itinerant state, not beggars and not even of the lowest working class: at some stage the man has earned enough to dress himself and his family respectably. In fact, it soon turns out that he is a skilled craftsman, and this fact too is communicated not by direct statement but by a visual detail. The 'rush basket' containing a 'hay-knife' and 'a wimble for hay-bonds' very precisely indicates his occupation as a hay-trusser, and this position in the social/occupational hierarchy finds further expression in his manner of walking: he has 'the walk of the skilled countryman' rather than 'the desultory shamble of the general labourer'.

Hardy deploys these details of dress, tools and other matters with authority: he is clearly writing of a world he knows intimately, and if we want to know, for instance, how a man of this type dressed in this period, his novels are a reliable source of information.

These details, and other similar ones, are interesting in two ways. They place the characters, even at this very early stage, quite firmly in a highly specific social world. But they also establish a narrative method that, as already noted in Chapter 1, is distinctively Hardyan. This is no 'omniscient narrator', speaking with God-like knowledge of all that concerns the fictional world, including matters of which the characters themselves may be unaware. The Hardyan narrator (not quite consistently, but strikingly often) is much more like a keen-eyed and well-informed observer – one might at times say *voyeur* – who sees, interprets and records very largely on the basis of visible signs. Another way of making this point is to liken the narrator to a detective, whose profession (perhaps significantly) emerged in the nineteenth century. It is difficult to discuss the technique of a passage such as this one without using some such term as 'pictorialism': though Hardy is a verbal rather than a graphic artist, he devotes a remarkable amount of creative energy to enabling the reader to form mental pictures.

This picture-making is aided and sharpened by what one is, again, tempted to call photographic detail. The man is, for instance, not merely wearing a hat but 'a straw hat overlaid with black glazed canvas'; not merely wearing a waistcoat but 'a fustian waistcoat with white horn buttons'. (Fustian, a hard-wearing material traditionally favoured by the working classes, again serves as a marker of status: the garment is not one that a 'gentleman' would ever have worn, or even a rising professional man such as Farfrae, Henchard's rival in the main action of the novel.) The particularity of such phrases belongs partly to the realistic tradition and can be paralleled in innumerable passages of, for example, Dickens or George Eliot; but they also reinforce the sense of a narrator who is looking as intently at the figure being described as would an artist who is about to paint him.

While 'pictures' of this kind are often 'stills' – and we recall at this point both Hardy's strong interest in the visual arts, and also the rapid development of the art of photography during his lifetime – they are also at times cinematic, as in the description of the man's mode of walking. There is even an instance of what might be regarded as 'close-up' in the curious detail of the folds in the man's loose trousers changing as he walks. But this is, as so often in Hardy, not just descriptive detail for its own sake but a means of depicting character: just as the man's face betrays his nature, his way of walking along the road, and even the folds in his clothing, reveal 'a dogged and cynical indifference personal to himself'. Our inner natures, Hardy seems to be saying, are inscribed in visual signs of all kinds, including faces, costume and mode of walking, and these signs can be 'read' by the skilled observer.

Before giving us this revealing 'close-up', the camera-eye of Hardy's narrator has captured an image of the whole group seen from a distance and has then 'zoomed in' to enable the reader's own visual imagination to take account of specific details. To pursue the cinematic parallel a little further, these opening paragraphs, depicting a series of visual images before a single word is spoken, may be compared to a pre-credit sequence in a modern film. Such scenes are common in Hardy's fiction, which often resorts to such basic motifs as a wide and almost empty landscape traversed by a road along which one or more figures are slowly moving.

The narrator is such an observer, making bridges between the world of the novel and the less observant or less well-informed reader. But in this passage at least, the narrator, though well qualified for the detective-like role of observer and interpreter, is not especially privileged and is certainly far from omniscient: when it comes to giving a reason for the man's behaviour in reading as he walks rather than talking to his wife, 'nobody but himself could have said precisely'. This is a significantly different narratorial stance from that of most nineteenth-century novelists. Hardy's characters, it seems, have a secret life that is not only unknown to their fellow-characters but inaccessible to the narrator and ultimately unknowable by the reader.

It is, too, unexpectedly and rather ominously, a *silent* picture. The three figures, as the narrator rather cynically indicates, obviously constitute a family, but there is no communication between husband and wife, and the former's reading seems no more than a device to avoid conversation. This is, in other words, an eloquent and unnatural silence that bespeaks something wrong inthe relationship. The silence is preserved until very near the end of the passage, when the sounds of activity indicate that they are approaching a village. The man's first utterance is a terse indication that he is seeking employment and thereby provides a reason for the family's itinerant state.

In a few paragraphs, then, Hardy has established time and place, begun to delineate the individual natures of two of his chief characters, and set the plot in motion – for it is in the village that the man (still unnamed) will take the most decisive step of his life, a step that follows directly from the incompatibility in the marriage relationship that has already been hinted at. Anyone reading these opening paragraphs is in no doubt that the main focus of the story that is to follow will be upon human experience: from the outset these figures, both individual and stereotypical, are placed in the context of family and work, the two elements that for most people constitute the main fabric of their lives. At the same time, as they travel the road between communities, they exist temporarily between two worlds, the one they have left behind (antecedent to the present story) and the one that they are heading towards. As they travel along the dusty road, our eyes travel along the lines of print and our minds anticipate the story that lies ahead, which, like an unfolding landscape, will have its own landmarks and surprises.

Far from the Madding Crowd: a 'rural painting'

We can get a stronger sense of the originality of the opening of *The Mayor of Casterbridge* by comparing it with the way in which Hardy had opened *Far from the Madding Crowd* a dozen years earlier in his career. Though the two passages have, as we shall see, certain common elements, suggesting that aspects of Hardy's technique were established quite early in his career, there are also radical differences of method and tone. Here is the opening of the first chapter, titled 'Description of Farmer Oak – An Incident', in the earlier novel:

> When Farmer Oak smiled, the corners of his mouth spread till they were within an unimportant distance of his ears, his eyes were reduced to chinks, and diverging wrinkles appeared round them, extending upon his countenance like the rays in a rudimentary sketch of the rising sun.
>
> His Christian name was Gabriel, and on working days he was a young man of sound judgement, easy motions, proper dress, and general good character. On Sundays he was a man of misty views, rather given to postponing, and hampered by his best clothes and umbrella: upon the whole, one who felt himself to occupy morally that vast middle space of Laodicean neutrality which lay between the Communion people of the parish and the drunken section – that is, he went to church, but yawned privately by the time the congregation reached the Nicene creed, and thought of what there would be for dinner when he meant to be listening to the sermon. Or, to state his character as it stood in the scale of public opinion, when his friends and critics were in tantrums, he was considered rather a bad man; when they were pleased, he was

rather a good man; when they were neither, he was a man whose moral colour was a kind of pepper-and-salt mixture.

Since he lived six times as many working days as Sundays, Oak's appearance in his old clotches was most peculiarly his own – the mental picture formed by his neighbours in imagining him being always dressed in that way. He wore a low-crowned felt that, spread out at the base by tight jamming upon the head for security in high winds, and a coat like Dr Johnson's, his lower extremities being encased in ordinary leather leggings and boots emphatically large, affording to each foot a roomy apartment so constructed that any wearer might stand in a river all day long and know nothing of damp – their maker being a conscientious man who endeavoured to compensate for any weakness in his cut by unstinted dimension and solidity.

Mr Oak carried about him, by way of watch, what may be called a small silver clock; in other words, it was a watch as to shape and intention, and a small clock as to size. This instrument being several years older than Oak's grandfather, had the peculiarity of going either too fast or not at all. The smaller of its hands, too, occasionally slipped round on the pivot, and thus, though the minutes were told with precision, nobody could be quite certain of the hour they belonged to. The stopping peculiarity of his watch Oak remedied by thumps and shakes, and he escaped any evil consequences from the other two defects by constant comparisons with and observations of the sun and stars, and by pressing his face close to the glass of his neighbours' windows, till he could discern the hour marked by the green-faced timekeepers within. It may be mentioned that Oak's fob being difficult of access, by reason of its somewhat high situation in the waistband of his trousers (which also lay at a remote height under his waistcoat), the watch was as a necessity pulled out by throwing the body to one side, compressing the mouth and face to a mere mass of ruddy flesh on account of the exertion, and drawing up the watch by its chain, like a bucket from a well.

But some thoughtful persons, who had seen him walking across one of his fields on a certain December morning – sunny and exceedingly mild – might have regarded Gabriel Oak in other aspects than these....

(Chapter 1)

Like the previous passage discussed, this introduces a working man who will turn out to be the hero of the story; but this time he is presented as a solitary figure rather than as a member of a group. Michael Henchard is shown at the outset as husband and father because he will very shortly abdicate these roles by committing the act of headstrong folly that will determine his future. Gabriel Oak, on the other hand, will remain single and in many ways a rather lonely figure until, right at the end, he succeeds in winning Bathsheba. From a technical point of view, there is also a strong contrast between the two passages. Whereas the opening of the *Mayor* works by hints, suggestions and implications that create an air of mystery, the opening of *Far from the Madding Crowd* is direct and explicit. Henchard is not named, but Gabriel's name is given in the novel's opening lines (his surname in its opening phrase). It is, however, a symbolic at least as much as a realistic name: Gabriel, with its angelic associations, suggests the hero's innate goodness and sweetness of temper (Hardy was later to use the name Angel ironically for Tess's husband), whereas Oak contrastingly implies the soundness and durability of a wood traditionally regarded as essentially English.

We noted the strong visual element in the presentation of Henchard, and in this earlier novel much of the same applies. Hardy's second published novel, *Under the Greenwood Tree*, had been subtitled 'A Rural Painting of the Dutch School', and though *Far from the Madding Crowd* is a much longer and more ambitious novel, that phrase could equally well be applied to its opening description. The 'Dutch School' referred to is the school of seventeenth-century painters such as Vermeer and Teniers who faithfully and lovingly depicted, in a highly realistic vein and with considerable attention to detail, humble characters and scenes from common life. Hardy had seen pictures of this kind in the National Gallery in London and elsewhere, and to a significant extent his prose attempts a verbal equivalent of such styles of visual art.

It is worth pausing for a moment to elaborate the point just made, since the visual or pictorial element in Hardy's work is of major importance. It goes without saying that literary discourse and such plastic arts as painting and sculpture are so entirely different in their nature that we can only speak very loosely of one 'imitating' the other. But just as we can speak of certain styles of visual art (for example, the paintings by members of the Pre-Raphaelite Brotherhood, formed while Hardy was still a child) as 'literary', there are certain novelists and poets whose work is strongly 'pictorial'. At the same time it must always be remembered that the processes of reading a literary text and 'reading' a painting are radically different: the nature of language, and hence of literary discourse, is linear, and our reading of a text is determined by syntax and printing conventions, but we have much more freedom, many more options, in scanning a picture and taking in the details that, for example, a Pre-Raphaelite painting, or one of the 'Dutch School', may offer. What Hardy does is to encourage us to form mental pictures by giving vivid details of the visual appearance of characters and scenes – here, for example, in the description (in the opening sentence) of the way Gabriel's face is transformed by smiling. He can also direct us to certain angles of vision, rather in the way that a film director will place a camera so as to draw attention to certain features of a figure or scene; and for this reason Hardy's art has sometimes been described (again rather loosely) as cinematic. His novels were all written before the invention of the cinema, but it may be significant that some of them were quickly adapted for the silent cinema when it emerged. It may be relevant, too, that his lifetime also saw an immense development in the art of photography. Other obvious examples of visual presentation include the account of Oak's dress in the third paragraph, while the description of his watch in the fourth may be compared to a cinematic close-up.

This visual technique is balanced by a prose that often has recourse to generalizations and abstractions. Thus the opening sentence of the second paragraph offers indications as to the character's moral nature rather than his outward appearance, and does so through such phrases as 'sound judgement' and 'general good character'. There is an obvious assumption that readers will share the narrator's standards and values in this and other respects: 'good character' is a rather vague term, and its precise meaning may be very much open to debate, but the implication here is that there is a general consensus among right-thinking people. Another kind of community of ideas that is taken for granted is represented by the allusions to, for instance, 'Laodicean neutrality', 'the Nicene creed' and 'a coat like Dr Johnson's'. Here what is in question is a shared culture of a highly conservative kind. Long before he wrote *Far from the Madding Crowd*, Hardy had abandoned the Christian faith in which he had been brought up, but this does not prevent him from making wide use of allusions to the Bible, the Prayer Book, and to Christian culture in general. (The term 'Laodicean', meaning indifferent or lukewarm in matters of religion, is derived from the Book of Revelation, and Hardy was later to write a novel titled *A Laodicean*; the Nicene creed is part of the Anglican service of Holy Communion.) Dr Johnson is one of the most famous personalities in English literature, and any educated reader would have seen representations of him in books or magazines.

This sense of a shared culture and morality implies a socially and educationally homogeneous readership, and there is a strong implication that this is a largely urban readership. The patronizing tone adopted towards the country tailor referred to at the end of the third paragraph, for instance, suggests a city- or town-dweller's view of rural society: country folk are ignorant and perhaps even stupid, but this is a matter for amused indulgence rather than reproach. Of course this was very far from being Hardy's own view, and his intimate knowledge of country life as well as his respect for the skills of country-dwellers is fully evident in many passages of this novel: Gabriel Oak is a man who not only can tell the time by looking at the stars but can perform an emergency operation on a dying animal, and in many other ways is a master of diverse crafts. Still, the tone of this opening passage remains one of humour in which the narrator and reader are distanced from the world inhabited by the characters. Even Gabriel, who will turn out to be the novel's hero, is at this stage something of a figure of fun, and this element in his presentation persists to some extent – for instance, in the comic accounts of his social ineptitude.

Though Gabriel is depicted as an individual, there is in this passage a strong sense of community (an aspect of Hardy's work that will be considered in greater detail in Chapter 4). He is defined partly in terms of his status as a farmer, with the social and economic implications carried by that status; this is a point of considerable importance, since Gabriel's fortunes in the course of the novel are to fluctuate dramatically and his status and occupation will undergo dramatic changes. It is made perfectly clear, too, that the community in question is both stable and Christian. Gabriel is not a man of any great spirituality, but it never occurs to him that he might fail to go to church, and his neighbours would be puzzled and perhaps scandalized if he were to do so. Especially in his later novels, Hardy is to be much concerned with communities whose stability is threatened or undermined, and even in *Far from the Madding Crowd* the glamorous and somewhat exotic figure of Sergeant Troy is a disturbing factor. But at the outset the emphasis is on stability and conformity.

The narrator's manner is somewhat formal but also leisurely and expansive: the description of Gabriel's watch, for example, is inflated in a way that suggests that a story beginning in this fashion will be a lengthy one. The tone is predominantly facetious, serious terms being deflated by association with commonplace ideas ('a man whose *moral colour* was *a kind of pepper-and-salt mixture*'; italics added). This opening passage is somewhat static: only at the end of the section quoted, with the reference to a specific time ('a certain December morning'), are we given the sense that a story is about to begin.

Jude the Obscure: the Uses of Realism

A good example of Hardy's use of realistic dialogue can be found at the end of *Jude the Obscure*. After Jude's death, two women talk quietly in the presence of his body, in a scene that is conceived in dramatic terms, complete with 'noises off'. The passage that follows is the last part of the novel's final chapter:

> Two days later, when the sky was equally cloudless, and the air equally still, two persons stood beside Jude's open coffin in the same little bedroom. On one side was Arabella, on the other the Widow Edlin. They were both looking at Jude's face, the worn old eyelids of Mrs Edlin being red.
>
> 'How beautiful he is!' said she.
>
> 'Yes. He's a 'andsome corpse,' said Arabella.
>
> The window was still open to ventilate the room, and it being about noontide the clear air was motionless and quiet without. From a

distance came voices; and an apparent noise of persons stamping.

'What's that?' murmured the old woman.

'Oh, that's the doctors in the Theatre, conferring Honorary degrees on the Duke of Hamptonshire and a lot more illustrious gents of that sort. It's Remembrance Week, you know. The cheers come from the young men.'

'Ay; young and strong-lunged! Not like our poor boy here.'

An occasional word, as from some one making a speech, floated from the open windows of the Theatre across to this quiet corner, at which there seemed to be a smile of some sort upon the marble features of Jude; while the old, superseded, Delphin editions of Virgil and Horace, and the dog-eared Greek Testament on the neighbouring shelf, and the few other volumes of the sort that he had not parted with, roughened with stone-dust where he had been in the habit of catching them up for a few minutes between his labours, seemed to pale to a sickly cast at the sounds. The bells struck out joyously; and their reverberations travelled round the bedroom.

Arabella's eyes removed from Jude to Mrs Edlin. 'D'ye think she will come?' she asked.

'I could not say. She swore not to see him again.'

'How is she looking?'

'Tired and miserable, poor heart. Years and years older than when you saw her last. Quite a staid, worn woman now. 'Tis the man; – she can't stomach un, even now!'

'If Jude had been alive to see her, he would hardly have cared for her any more, perhaps.'

'That's what we don't know ... Didn't he ever ask you to send for her, since he came to see her in that strange way?'

'No. Quite the contrary. I offered to send, and he said I was not to let her know how ill he was.'

'Did he forgive her?'

'Not as I know.'

'Well – poor little thing, 'tis to be believed she's found happiness somewhere! She said she had found peace!'

'She may swear that on her knees to the holy cross on her necklace till she's hoarse, but it won't be true!' said Arabella. 'She's never found peace since she left his arms, and never will again till she's as he is now!'

(Part VI, Chapter 11)

As the opening phrase 'Two days later' suggests, this passage constitutes a kind of coda or epilogue to the novel. The chapter of which it forms the conclusion has begun with a warning to the reader that a conclusion is imminent: 'The last pages to which the chronicler of these lives would ask the reader's attention are concerned with the scene in and out of Jude's bedroom when leafy summer came round again.' *Jude the Obscure* has sometimes been described as the first modern novel, but Hardy is resolutely traditional both in giving this warning and in phrasing it in a manner that draws attention to the narrator and the audience, the act of writing and the act of reading. He is, moreover, presenting it as a distinctly old-fashioned kind of narrative, a 'chronicle' or more or less objective history. The reference to 'leafy summer' is both part of a clear chronology – for this is a novel that traces the hero's fortunes from childhood to death – and also part of a pattern of seasonal symbolism. When Jude has paid his last visit to Sue, the bad weather has been both realistic and symbolic, affecting Jude's worsening health and also mirroring the turbulence of his emotions: now, in 'leafy summer', the symbolism is ironic, since Jude's 'leaf' is doomed to fall prematurely.

The chapter has gone on to describe Jude's solitary death, with a counterpointing, again ironic, of the scenes 'in and out of Jude's bedroom'. Outside, the academic festivities of the university city are in full swing, for this is the end of the academic year, and there is a background chorus of cheering that will be commented on in the chapter's closing lines. Inside, Jude is quoting the terrible words of the Book of Job and, with his dying breath, cursing the day on which he was born. Part of the irony of the situation is that Jude, close enough to the privileged world of Christminster to hear distinctly the sounds of the 'Remembrance games', remains excluded from that world in death as he has been in life.

In the passage quoted above, two women discuss Jude's life and death, and again we may see this as an ironic, almost parodic, version of the funeral oration or memorial address delivered in honour of someone who has achieved more success in life than has been within Jude's reach. The speakers are both uneducated women, and neither has a complete command of Standard English, but Hardy draws a careful distinction between them: the Widow Edlin's simplicity and good nature find expression in genuine grief and pity that do not quite exclude a tendency to sentimentalize the true situation, whereas Arabella, more canny and tough-minded, sees the situation as it really is.

Notice the marked difference of tone between the deathbed scene and what has already been described as the coda or epilogue that follows it. The bitter contrast between the fate of Jude, who dies in a state of despair, and the gaiety of the privileged ones is underlined by the different and alternating voices: inside the room, Jude utters what amounts to a terrible curse on his own destiny, in the resounding language of the Old Testament, while the thoroughly contemporary scene outside makes itself heard through the window. The technique recalls the use of the 'chorus' in Greek tragedy, whereby the dramatic action is counterpointed by a commentary often ironic in nature. The scene between the two women, on the other hand, is more muted and restrained: instead of a stark contrast between happiness and misery, there is a sober and relatively objective assessment of the situation. In these closing lines, Fate now seems indifferent to human lives, whereas in the deathbed scene some positively hostile and malicious force seemed to be at work to deprive Jude of any last-minute consolation.

The dialogue given to the two women is realistic, at moments even banal, with mostly short sentences and an everyday vocabulary, and the scene as a whole, with its presentation of the corpse lying in the shabby room, has the sober, uncompromising realism that has been characteristic of a large part of the novel, from the first chapter onwards. Consider, for instance, the implications of the detail that the window was open 'to ventilate the room'. In the Victorian period (and, indeed, long afterwards), the dead normally remained in the home until burial, and in summer putrefaction would be evident after two days. At the same time the low-keyed conversation, which rises to rhetoric only in Arabella's concluding words, touches on some of the most important issues of the novel.

Within the linguistically narrow limits of the dialogue, the vocabulary and syntax of which reflect the intellectual and social background of the two speakers, Hardy differentiates effectively between them. As they both look at Jude's body, the Widow Edlin expresses a spontaneous and impersonal sentiment – 'How beautiful he is!' –

whereas Arabella's 'He's a 'andsome corpse' reminds the reader of her sensuality as well as her capacity for looking facts squarely in the face and not mincing words: for her Jude can still be looked at as if he were a sexual object, but is undeniably dead. Again, it is the Widow who wistfully draws attention to the melancholy contrast between the 'strong-lunged' young men who, very much alive, are shouting outside and the dead man, still quite young, whose weak lungs, not much helped by poor diet and housing, have been among the causes of his death. For her part, Arabella can scarcely conceal a kind of grim satisfaction at hearing the news that Sue has lost her looks under the pressures of her misery ('If Jude had been alive to see her, he would hardly have cared for her any more, perhaps'): even though Jude is dead, in Arabella's eyes Sue is still a sexual rival.

This dialogue occupies most of the concluding pages, but there is one passage that draws attention, in a way that is highly characteristic of Hardy's pictorial art, to details in the sparse furnishings of the room. We are given a 'cinematic' close-up of the few shabby books on his shelves, out of date and bearing the marks of his occupation as a stonemason, but still potent emblems of the ambitions that have fired him but have never reached fulfilment. The paragraph that refers to them begins and ends with allusions to the life of the university that was denied to Jude, so that these silent and pathetic reminders of his vain struggles acquire all the more force by contrast with the cheerful noises coming through the window.

It may be said that the story told in *Jude the Obscure* effectively concludes with the death of the protagonist, so that it is appropriate to ask what function is served by this coda or epilogue. A relevant comparison is with Shakespearean tragedy, where typically (as in, for example, *Hamlet* and *Macbeth*) the death of the protagonist is followed by a passage that affirms continuity and promises a fresh start, very often through the agency of a minor character. Hardy's tragic fictions were deeply influenced by the Shakespearean model – indeed, part of his contribution to the tradition of the novel was to extend the boundaries of the realistic novel by infusing into it certain elements of the tragic drama – and in this instance he conforms quite closely to this pattern. The most important relationship in the novel has been that between Jude and Sue, but Sue makes no direct appearance after his death, and in these final pages is not even named, though she is very much in the thoughts of the lesser characters who comment, chorus-like, on her present and future state. For her part Sue is trapped, self-punishingly, in a loveless marriage with Phillotson. The Widow Edlin's optimistic and sentimental confidence that Sue has 'found forgiveness somewhere' and 'found peace' is flatly contradicted by the clear-eyed Arabella, and the contradiction carries conviction. The effect of Arabella's final words is to turn the spotlight from Jude onto Sue – indeed they represent a kind of advance epitaph for Sue, who may still have decades of misery to endure before death brings her peace. In this respect the ending of *Jude* may be compared with that of both *Tess* and *The Mayor*, where the final focus shifts from the protagonist, now distanced by death and already, as it were, half-forgotten, to the living, who must continue to carry what Hardy saw as the burdens of existence and consciousness.

Quietly but firmly, this short passage has brought together the main themes of the novel: Jude's dogged quest for an education; the failure of his academic ambitions; his exclusion by the elitism of an ancient university; the contrast between Sue's morbidly sensitive nature and fear of sex and Arabella's vigorous instinct for self-preservation and aggressive sexuality; and the bitter criticism of the institution of marriage, as interpreted in late nineteenth-century England, whereby Sue has felt compelled to abandon the genuinely loving relationship she had with Jude in favour of cohabitation with a husband who, as the old woman bluntly puts it, she 'can't stomach'.

That the setting of this final scene should be 'Christminster', which has played so prominent a role from an early stage of the novel, and to which, as both symbol and actuality, Jude has repeatedly returned, is entirely appropriate. To some extent the construction of Hardy's novel is cyclic: from time to time Jude seems to be making progress in his life – in his studies and academic ambitions, for instance, or in his emotional relationships with women – but the hardships and unfairness of his condition, and the sensitivity and vulnerability of his nature, wipe out this progress and cause his fortunes to plunge. One result of this is that he keeps returning to the same place, situation or relationship: having started in the bakery business, he returns to it near the end of his life; having freed himself from

Arabella, he returns to her; and having dreamed of Christminster as a boy and suffered heartbreak as a young man from its rejection of his legitimate aspirations, he goes back there to die.

Tess of the d'Urbervilles: the Case of the Disappearing Heroine

The ending of *Tess of the d'Urbervilles* has elements in common with that of *Jude*, but there are also some significant differences. What follows is the whole of the novel's short final chapter:

> The city of Wintoncester, that fine old city, aforetime capital of Wessex, lay amidst its convex and concave downlands in all the brightness and warmth of a July morning. The gabled brick, tile, and freestone houses had almost dried off for the season their integument of lichen, the streams in the meadows were low, and in the sloping High Street, from the West Gateway to the mediaeval cross, and from the mediaeval cross to the bridge, that leisurely dusting and sweeping was in progress which usually ushers in an old-fashioned market-day.
>
> From the western gate aforesaid the highway, as every Wintoncestrian knows, ascends a long and regular incline of the exact length of a measured mile, leaving the houses gradually behind. Up this road from the precincts of the city two persons were walking rapidly, as if unconscious of the trying ascent – unconscious through preoccupation and not through buoyancy. They had emerged upon this road through a narrow barred wicket in a high wall a little lower down. They seemed anxious to get out of the sight of the houses and of their kind, and this road appeared to offer the quickest means of doing so. Though they were young they walked with bowed heads, which gait of grief the sun's rays smiled on pitilessly.
>
> One of the pair was Angel Clare, the other a tall budding creature – half girl, half woman – a spiritualized image of Tess, slighter than she, but with the same beautiful eyes – Clare's sister-in-law, 'Liza-Lu. Their pale faces seemed to have shrunk to half their natural size. They moved on hand in hand, and never spoke a word, the drooping of their heads being that of Giotto's 'Two Apostles'.
>
> When they had nearly reached the top of the great West Hill the clocks in the town struck eight. Each gave a start at the notes, and,

walking onward yet a few steps, they reached the first milestone, standing whitely on the green margin of the grass, and backed by the down, which here was open to the road. They entered upon the turf, and, impelled by a force that seemed to overrule their will, suddenly stood still, turned, and waited in paralysed suspense beside the stone.

The prospect from this summit was almost unlimited. In the valley beneath lay the city they had just left, its more prominent buildings showing as in an isometric drawing – among them the broad cathedral tower, with its Norman windows and immense length of aisle and nave, the spires of St Thomas's, the pinnacled tower of the College, and, more to the right, the tower and gables of the ancient hospice where to this day the pilgrim may receive his dole of bread and ale. Behind the city swept the rotund upland of St Catherine's Hill; further off, landscape beyond landscape, till the horizon was lost in the radiance of the sun hanging above it.

Against these far stretches of country rose, in front of the other city edifices, a large red-brick building with level gray roofs, and rows of short barred windows bespeaking captivity, the whole contrasting greatly by its formalism with the quaint irregularities of the Gothic erections. It was somewhat disguised from the road in passing it by yews and evergreen oaks, but it was visible enough up here. The wicket from which the pair had lately emerged was in the wall of this structure. From the middle of the building an ugly flat-topped octagonal tower ascended against the east horizon, and viewed from this spot, on its shady side and against the light, it seemed the one blot on the city's beauty. Yet it was with this blot, and not with the beauty, that the two gazers were concerned.

Upon the cornice of the tower a tall staff was fixed. Their eyes were riveted on it. A few minutes after the hour had struck something moved slowly up the staff, and extended itself upon the breeze. It was a black flag.

'Justice' was done, and the President of the Immortals, in Aeschylean phrase, had ended his sport with Tess. And the d'Urberville knights and dames slept on in their tombs unknowing. The two speechless gazers bent themselves down to the earth, as if in prayer, and remained thus a long time, absolutely motionless: the flag continued to wave silently. As soon as they had strength they arose, joined hands again, and went on.

(Chapter 59)

What is striking about the opening of this final chapter is the objectivity and dispassionateness of the narratorial voice, whose tone is rather that of the guidebook than of a work of imaginative fiction. Phrases like 'that fine old city' and 'the mediaeval cross', and formal and archaic terms such as 'aforetime' and 'aforesaid', like the later reference to an 'isometric drawing', imply a speaker with certain specialized knowledge and interests (antiquarian, topographical, architectural) but no reason to show a personal or emotional interest in the scene – and also imply the assumption that the reader's interest is likely to be of a similar kind. When the human figures are introduced, they are not at first named (a strategy we have already noted in the opening of *The Mayor of Casterbridge*), and the nature of the building from which they emerge is not divulged. Hardy is bringing to a conclusion a story of joy and suffering, intense feelings and tragic events, but at this point he, or at least his narrator, seems curiously detached from it all.

This is, as we might guess from a great novelist at the height of his powers, a carefully contrived sleight of hand. Hardy's task is to confront his readers with something almost unbearably painful: the death by hanging, or judicial murder, of his heroine, who from any reasonable and humane point of view is herself a victim rather than a wrongdoer. We have seen already that in narrating the murder of Alec (discussed on p. 21 above), Hardy resorts to a narrative point of view that permits only indirect access to Tess's actions and none at all to her feelings. Consistently with this strategy of indirection, he now, at least initially, gives his narrator a tone that is objective almost to the point of blandness, and depersonalizes the 'two persons' soon to be identified as Angel Clare and Tess's younger sister, 'Liza-Lu. Before the end of the chapter the narrator will have exchanged this objectivity for a very different tone, angry and ironic, and the swing from the sedate opening to the provocative and impassioned final paragraph is very powerful.

In the description of the streets and public buildings of 'Wintoncester' (a city that closely resembles Winchester), we can find evidence of Hardy's architectural training and his lifelong interest in architecture. Here too there is irony in the contrast between the magnificent buildings created by past ages, such as the cathedral, and the stark, utilitarian prison, 'the one blot on the city's beauty' and a creation of his own time (the first sentence of the paragraph beginning 'Against these far stretches...' makes the contrast explicit, and indeed uses the word 'contrasting'). The point being made is not, however, simply an architectural or aesthetic one: the humanitarian purposes of the 'ancient hospice', a charitable foundation still functioning in the modern age, is set in contrast with the repressive heartlessness of a penal system that can execute a young woman who, as Hardy challengingly insists on the novel's title-page, is essentially 'pure' and innocent.

Tess's fate is not, however, referred to until quite near the end of the chapter: it is only in the sixth paragraph that we learn that the building from which Angel and his companion have emerged is in fact the prison. We may like to assume that they have paid a farewell visit to Tess, but this is nowhere stated. The word 'prison' is never in fact used. Nor, more importantly, is the fact of the execution stated: it is signalled, for the two spectators and for the reader, by the hoisting of the 'black flag' – at first only a 'something' – laconically announced at the end of the penultimate paragraph. Earlier in the chapter, Hardy has given a clue that might be picked up by an astute reader. When the clocks strike eight, Angel and his companion react in an unexpected manner, and Victorian readers would be aware that executions normally took place at that hour of the morning. But the significant point is that Tess's death is narrated by hints and implications rather than by direct statement. To say 'Tess suffered death by hanging' would be – or so Hardy seems to judge – too crude to be acceptable to himself or his readers.

The distinctive nature of Hardy's narrative art becomes clear if we consider what a novelist more inclined to dramatic, even melodramatic, effects might have done with this final episode. Dickens, for example, might have taken us into the condemned cell (as he does before the execution of Fagin in *Oliver Twist*), even onto the scaffold (as he does at the end of *A Tale of Two Cities*, where we stand imaginatively beside his hero as he faces the guillotine). As already suggested in Chapter 1, Hardy's fictional practice may well have been influenced by his deep knowledge of the tragic drama of ancient Greece, in which violent action takes place offstage – a principle that Hardy seems to have transferred to the realistic novel. (For other examples, consider the deaths of Eustacia Vye and Damon Wildeve in *The Return of the Native*, also that of Michael Henchard and, earlier, his wife Susan in *The Mayor of Casterbridge*.)

Another distancing device that is also very characteristic is the allusion to an Old Master painting: '...the drooping of their heads being that of Giotto's "Two Apostles"'. This reference is not likely to mean very much to a reader who is not familiar with the painting in question (now in fact believed to be not by Giotto but by another artist of the period, Spinello Aretino). But Hardy takes for granted a shared culture, assuming that his readers, many of whom would live in London or at least be on nodding terms with the London art-collections, have seen the picture in the National Gallery, as he himself had done.

A less explicit allusion, in the final words of the passage, is to the closing lines of Milton's *Paradise Lost* (a poem widely familiar to educated Victorian readers), where Adam and Eve 'hand in hand, with wandering steps and slow, / Through Eden took their solitary way'. Some readers take the view that Hardy wishes us to understand that Angel and 'Liza-Lu will marry, and this would certainly be consistent with his Shakespearean tendency to affirm continuity and a more or less stable future beyond the conclusion of the narrative. If we are to take the Miltonic parallel seriously, however, it is important to bear in mind that by the end of Milton's poem Adam and Eve have been expelled from Paradise, and this inevitably casts a tragic tinge over any future that the two survivors may have after Tess's death.

The final paragraph of the novel proved, for many of its earliest readers and critics, one of the most controversial and even offensive passages in a controversial and offensive book. The particular source of offence was the first sentence of that paragraph, which quickly moves from an indictment of human justice, as institutionalized by the late Victorian penal code, to an attack upon the very grounds of Christian faith. The first of these targets is made explicit by the ironic quotation marks around 'Justice'. The second, however, is concealed under the allusion to a phrase used by the Greek tragic dramatist Aeschylus – a phrase here translated by Hardy as 'the President of the Immortals'.

The concealment was not successful enough to avoid giving offence, since many were ready to interpret this phrase as referring to the Christian God, and such an interpretation is indeed borne out by Hardy's consistent religious scepticism in his life and his writings. The manuscript of *Tess* shows that the allusion was an afterthought, and in the serial version of the novel published in the *Graphic* the sentence appeared in watered down form as ' "Justice" was done and Time, the Arch-satirist, had had his joke out with Tess.' There cannot be much doubt that the final version, followed by the less controversial but still moving irony of the reference to the indifference of 'the d'Urberville knights and dames', provides a more powerful ending, and one that is in style and tone a long way from the serene opening of the chapter only a few paragraphs earlier.

Conclusions

We have seen that Hardy's beginnings and endings display considerable variety and do not always conform to patterns traditional in nineteenth-century fiction. *The Mayor of Casterbridge* opens with the favourite Hardyan motif of people travelling along a road (compare, in this respect, *Tess of the d'Urbervilles* and *The Woodlanders*), but, as already noted, *The Return of the Native* works quite differently, establishing scene and mood rather than introducing character or inaugurating plot – in other words, functioning in a mode associated with poetry and poetic drama rather than realistic fiction. Even in the more traditional opening of *The Mayor*, the narrative method defines itself as idiosyncratic, the point of view being that of an observer whose knowledge is far from complete, rather than the traditional omniscient narrator.

The ending of *Jude* is highly realistic, its setting banal and its tone for the most part low-keyed, and is largely conducted through dialogue. *Tess*, on the other hand, ends with an entirely silent scene, realistic in its setting but with strong mythic overtones. Both of these conclusions reach a rhetorical climax in their closing lines; both draw together some of the main themes of their respective novels; and both look beyond the end of the text to lives that continue after the death of the protagonist.

A more general point is that Hardy habitually works through indirection and implication rather than direct statement: the reader is left to draw conclusions from the evidence provided (concerning, for instance, Henchard's character and mood, or Tess's end), and such devices as irony, symbolism and allusiveness all impose upon the reader an interpretative role.

Methods of Analysis

In this chapter the following elements have received particular attention:

1. Narrative point of view, to determine the stance and define the tone of the narrator (neither stance nor tone, of course, is necessarily consistent throughout a long work, and the shifts may themselves be of significance and interest).
2. Hardy's pictorialism, including his use of significant and suggestive descriptive detail to convey information about social, regional and occupational status (the account of Henchard and his family), to depict settings in which the architectural or other visual detail is often symbolic as well as realistic (as in the Wintoncester townscape at the end of *Tess*), to advance the narrative through signs rather than direct statements (the black flag that announces Tess's death), and to pick up elements from earlier stages of the story (Jude's worn textbooks, again functioning as symbols as well as commonplace objects).
3. Varieties of language used – narrative, description, commentary, dialogue – including the use of non-standard forms.
4. Allusions to literature, mythology, etc., which give a broader dimension to specific instances of human experience and often work through ironic contrast.

Suggestions for Further Work

As a further example of a novel-opening, consider the first two pages of *Tess of the d'Urbervilles*, as far as ' " ... had no doubt on the subject" '.

Among points for consideration are the following: What are the notable features of the opening sentence, how would you describe the narratorial tone, and what kind of fiction does this opening seem to promise? How can the dialogue that follows be said to be both trival and momentous? How are the 'voices' of the two speakers differentiated from each other, and also from the narrative 'voice'.

The short opening chapter of *Jude the Obscure* strikes a significant keynote, and it is worth considering its relationship to the story that follows. The emphasis on dislocation in the first paragraph seems to concern only the departure of a single individual (who has aspirations to upward mobility) from a settled community, but by the end of the chapter the community itself is shown to be the victim of intrusion and change. Notice, too, how Hardy conveys a sense of a hierarchical society in which each member (rector, blacksmith, etc.) has an acknowledged place, while at the same time he recognizes that change is inevitable. It is in this social and historical context that the young Jude is placed when the reader first encounters him.

The final chapter of *Far from the Madding Crowd* may be examined with the question in mind: How far has Hardy provided a 'happy ending' to gratify the conventional tastes of the readers of his serial, and how far does the marriage of Bathsheba and Gabriel raise questions rather than settling matters? Is this perhaps a conclusion that does not really conclude? Is the role now assigned to Bathsheba consistent with the way in which she has been characterized throughout the novel?

You may also like to look carefully at the ending of *The Mayor of Casterbridge*, from 'They stood in silence...' (just before 'MICHAEL HENCHARD'S WILL'). What impression is made on the reader by the content and language of Henchard's 'will'? Can you suggest reasons why Hardy may have chosen this means of giving an insight into Henchard's state of mind on the point of death, rather than (for instance) giving a dying speech or some account of his dying thoughts? What is the effect of filtering Henchard's end through Farfrae and Elizabeth-Jane, and why should the emphasis at the end fall on the latter?

3

Nature and Humanity

Introduction

Historically speaking, the idea of 'nature' underwent profound changes during the nineteenth century, largely as a result of the ways in which science radically modified perceptions of the natural world. For Wordsworth (a poet much admired by Hardy), at the beginning of the century, nature was a moral guide and a source of wholesome influences: humanity could and should live in harmony with nature. But Tennyson, at the mid-century, famously characterized nature as 'red in tooth and claw', with its creatures existing in a state of relentless and competitive savagery: humanity was admirable only in so far as it had risen above the brutal appetites of the natural world.

For Hardy, 'nature' could imply a number of different and even contradictory ideas. In the passages to be discussed in this chapter, we shall see that it can involve an external world deeply in sympathy with human activities and feelings, which in turn it helps to promote, but can also represent an environment that seems indifferent or even hostile to human desires and endeavours. Human survival can involve a struggle with the forces of nature, which can at times be terrifying and destructive; in a less dramatic way, the caprices of the natural world beyond human control can make or mar human fortunes. What nature rarely if ever amounts to in Hardy's fiction is mere 'background', an aesthetically pleasing or sentimentally gratifying backdrop to human lives, or a welcome if temporary escape from less congenial modes of existence. For Hardy the relationship between humanity and nature is always close, at least for the characters who are presented sympathetically. It is only morally suspect outsiders like Sergeant Troy and Alec d'Urberville who seem indifferent to the natural world and untouched by it.

Tess of the d'Urbervilles: 'impregnated by their surroundings'

The following passage portrays the gradual growth of love between Tess and Angel. This takes place not merely in the idyllic setting of Talbothays in the 'Valley of the Great Dairies', but at a time of year when the earth seems bursting with vitality and fertility. Human lives are shown as sharing the same impulses and rhythms as those of non-human and inanimate nature.

> Amid the oozing fatness and warm ferments of the Var Vale, at a season when the rush of juices could almost be heard below the hiss of fertilization, it was impossible that the most fanciful love should not grow passionate. The ready bosoms existing there were impregnated by their surroundings.
>
> July passed over their heads, and the Thermidorean weather which came in its wake seemed an effort on the part of Nature to match the state of hearts at Talbothays Dairy. The air of the place, so fresh in the spring and early summer, was stagnant and enervating now. Its heavy scents weighed upon them, and at mid-day the landscape seemed lying in a swoon. Ethiopic scorchings browned the upper slopes of the pastures, but there was still bright green herbage here where the watercourses purled. And as Clare was oppressed by the outward heats, so was he burdened inwardly by waxing fervour of passion for the soft and silent Tess.
>
> The rains having passed the uplands were dry. The wheels of the dairyman's spring-cart, as he sped home from market, licked up the pulverized surface of the highway, and were followed by white ribands of dust, as if they had set a thin powder-train on fire. The cows jumped wildly over the five-barred barton-gate, maddened by the gad-fly; Dairyman Crick kept his shirt-sleeves permanently rolled up from Monday to Saturday; open windows had no effect in ventilation with-

out open doors, and in the dairy garden the blackbirds and thrushes crept about under the currant-bushes, rather in the manner of quadrupeds than of winged creatures. The flies in the kitchen were lazy, teasing, and familiar, crawling about in unwonted places, on the floor, into drawers, and over the backs of the milkmaids' hands. Conversations were concerning sunstroke; while butter-making, and still more butter-keeping, was a despair.

They milked entirely in the meads for coolness and convenience, without driving in the cows. During the day the animals obsequiously followed the shadow of the smallest tree as it moved round the stem with the diurnal roll; and when the milkers came they could hardly stand still for the flies.

On one of these afternoons four or five unmilked cows chanced to stand apart from the general herd, behind the corner of a hedge, among them being Dumpling and Old Pretty, who loved Tess's hands above those of any other maid. When she rose from her stool under a finished cow Angel Clare, who had been observing her for some time, asked her if she would take the aforesaid creatures next. She silently assented, and with her stool at arm's length, and the pail against her knee, went round to where they stood. Soon the sound of Old Pretty's milk fizzing into the pail came through the hedge, and then Angel felt inclined to go round the corner also, to finish off a hard-yielding milcher who had strayed there, he being now as capable of this as the dairyman himself.

All the men, and some of the women, when milking, dug their foreheads into the cows and gazed into the pail. But a few – mainly the younger ones – rested their heads sideways. This was Tess Durbeyfield's habit, her temple pressing the milcher's flank, her eyes fixed on the far end of the meadow with the quiet of one lost in meditation. She was milking Old Pretty thus, and the sun chancing to be on the milking-side it shone flat upon her pink-gowned form and her white curtain-bonnet, and upon her profile, rendering it keen as a cameo cut from the dun background of the cow.

She did not know that Clare had followed her round, and that he sat under his cow watching her. The stillness of her head and features was remarkable: she might have been in a trance, her eyes open, yet unseeing. Nothing in the picture moved but Old Pretty's tail and Tess's pink hands, the latter so gently as to be a rhythmic pulsation only, as if they were obeying a reflex stimulus, like a beating heart.

(Chapter 24)

Although a couple of individual characters are referred to by name, the first half of this passage is concerned less with story and character than with place and season. As a setting – simultaneously symbolic and highly realistic – for the growing love of Tess and Angel, Hardy creates a picture of the region at the height of the season of fertility and growth. And yet 'picture' is not really an adequate term, since the appeal is to other senses as well as the visual. From the opening phrase, with the poetic reference to 'oozing fatness', the language is often sensuous. (In using this phrase Hardy was perhaps recalling the use of the word 'oozings' by Keats, one of his favourite poets, in his ode 'To Autumn'.) Human sexuality is thus depicted in the context of the natural and instinctive rhythms of growth and reproduction.

It needs to be said, however, that to refer to 'nature' in relation to this passage is not to use the word in quite the senses that Darwin or even Wordsworth would have had in mind. It is now generally recognized that the English countryside is not so much a product of 'nature' as the result of generations of human planning and shaping, and the fertile meadows surrounding Talbothays Dairy, like the domestic animals they nourish, represent a tamed and disciplined version of the natural world, controlled by and subjected to human requirements. At the same time, just as civilized human beings retain some of the instincts of their early ancestors, the impulses of growth and procreation – vividly referred to by Hardy as 'the rush of juices' – are as spontaneous and powerful as in a tropical jungle.

The opening paragraph places human desire firmly in relation to the wider natural world. The language, as we have seen, is poetic and sensuous, sometimes with strong sexual overtones. Words like 'rush' and 'hiss' are used not only for their prose meanings but for their sound-effects, and such terms as 'fertilization' and 'impregnated' seem to allude not only to botanical phenomena but also to human sexuality. In such a place, at such a time, Hardy suggests, 'it was impossible that the most fanciful love should not grow passionate', and the implied distinction between 'fancy' and 'passion' seems to be between mental and physical feelings – a mild attraction and a powerful urge that is physical as well as emotional.

In the second paragraph, Hardy himself introduces the word 'nature', stating explicitly that the hot weather 'seemed an effort on the part of Nature to match the state of hearts at Talbothays'. The narrator has already distanced himself from the world of the dairy farm by the use of the pedantic phrase 'Thermidorean weather' earlier in the same sentence ('Thermidor', meaning literally 'gift of heat', was the name given the period of late July and early August under the new calendar introduced in France after the 1789 Revolution). Perhaps, therefore, this suggestion that nature 'matches' or behaves in sympathy with human feelings should be taken as ironical. If taken literally, it seems to be an example of what the Victorian thinker John Ruskin referred to as the 'pathetic fallacy': the implication (as in the phrase 'cruel sea') that the natural world is capable of feelings, kindly or otherwise, towards humanity. Closer to the truth is the idea, frequently encountered elsewhere in Hardy's writings, that human feelings are subject to impulses that link them to the non-human world.

Whether 'pathetic fallacy' or not, Hardy stresses the interrelationship between the external and the internal: between, for instance, the weather and human emotions. In the last sentence of the second paragraph Angel is shown as 'oppressed' by a double burden, 'outward heats' and 'inwardly by waxing fervour of passion for the soft and silent Tess'. But the third paragraph turns aside for a moment from these individuals and is entirely descriptive. Through a listing of sharply-observed visual details of daily life outdoors and indoors, Hardy creates a picture of necessary work being done under exceptionally trying climatic conditions. This is an important point, for the story of the love of Angel and Tess is placed firmly in the world of work – which, on a dairy farm, inevitably occupies seven days a week.

It is appropriate, therefore, that the second half of the passage, in which the narrative focus draws much closer to the young lovers, should be set in the meadows where milking is taking place. A courtship ritual is being enacted, but it is necessarily subjected to the movements and actions of the lovers as they go about the routine business of milking the cows. Here again there is a highly sensuous dimension to the scene: we can imaginatively share the bodily experience of the milkers who 'dug their foreheads into the cows', and Hardy's choice of verb in the description of 'milk fizzing into the pail' encourages us to see and hear it. An interesting point is the charming and affectionate naming of the individual cows: these animals are not just elements in a business enterprise and machines for producing a saleable commodity, but, like household pets, part of the community. To name an animal is to give it an identity and a value beyond the commercial or utilitarian.

The pictorial aspect is, once again, strong in the account of Angel and Tess going about their tasks, and the word 'picture' is actually used in the final sentence of the excerpt. The detailed description of Tess's appearance at the end of the penultimate paragraph is especially striking. Notable here is the reference to 'her profile ... keen as a cameo'. The direct sunlight, illuminating Tess's face in profile against the 'dun' (dull brown) body of the cow, reminds Hardy of a cameo, a small-scale work of art made of precious or semi-precious stones carved to depict a figure in relief against a background of a different colour. The simile or analogy is visually close, but the associations of such an object with wealth, status and refined taste – the figure depicted would, typically, have been not a milkmaid but in classical style – are far removed from the world inhabited by Tess. Such images can therefore function thematically and even ironically as well as decoratively.

In the final sentence we are given a sense of the act of milking not merely as an idea but as a physical sensation: almost automatically, and as if she is 'in a trance', Tess's hands perform this familiar task. Her mind seems far away, as already suggested in the previous paragraph, where she seems 'lost in meditation', and these details recall the earlier reference to her as 'silent'. This aspect of her character reinforces the idea of Tess as a sufferer and a natural victim rather than the initiator of action – an idea that links her earlier treatment by Alec with her later treatment by Angel.

In this phase of the novel, then, nature and humanity seem in harmony: place and season conspire to produce the circumstances in which love and happiness can flourish. But just as the seasons inexorably change, such harmony does not last, and the later episode of Tess's experience under an unsympathetic employer at the upland arable farm of Flintcomb-Ash will stand in grim and ironic contrast to the short-lived Talbothays idyll.

Jude the Obscure: Landscape and Alienation

The following passage makes an interesting contrast with the one just discussed. Here the central figure is alone in a landscape that seems ugly and unfriendly, or at least indifferent to human feelings. Instead of being a member of a close-knit community, collaborating in congenial work, such as Tess was at Talbothays, Jude is isolated, lonely, and set to perform a monotonous task that he believes to be wrong.

> Jude, finding the general attention again centering on himself, went out to the bakehouse, where he ate the cake provided for his breakfast. The end of his spare time had now arrived, and emerging from the garden by getting over the hedge at the back he pursued a path northward, till he came to a wide and lonely depression in the general level of the upland, which was swon as a corn-field. This vast concave was the scene of his labours for Mr Troutham the farmer, and he descended into the midst of it.
>
> The brown surface of the field went right up towards the sky all round, where it was lost by degrees in the mist that shut out the actual verge and accentuated the solitude. The only marks on the uniformity of the scene were a rick of last year's produce standing in the midst of the arable, the rooks that rose at his approach, and the path athwart the fallow by which he had come, trodden now by he hardly knew whom, though once by many of his own dead family.
>
> 'How ugly it is here!' he murmured.
>
> The fresh harrow-lines seemed to stretch like the channellings in a piece of new corduroy, lending a meanly utilitarian air to the expanse, taking away its gradations, and depriving it of all history beyond that of the few recent months, though to every clod and stone there really attached associations enough and to spare – echoes of songs from ancient harvest-days, of spoken words, and of sturdy deeds. Every inch of ground had been the site, first or last, of energy, gaiety, horse-play, bickering, weariness. Groups of gleaners had squatted in the sun on

every square yard. Love-matches that had populated the adjoining hamlet had been made up there between reaping and carrying. Under the hedge which divided the field from a distant plantation girls had given themselves to lovers who would not turn their heads to look at them by the next harvest; and in that ancient cornfield many a man had made love-promises to a woman at whose voice he had trembled by the next seed-time after fulfilling them in the church adjoining. But this neither Jude nor the rooks around him considered. For them it was a lonely place, possessing, in the one view, only the quality of a work-ground, and in the other that of a granary good to feed in.

The boy stood under the rick before mentioned, and every few seconds used his clacker or rattle briskly. At each clack the rooks left off pecking, and rose and went away on their leisurely wings, burnished like tassets of mail, afterwards wheeling back and regarding him warily, and descending to feed at a more respectful distance.

He sounded the clacker till his arm ached, and at length his heart grew sympathetic with the birds' thwarted desires. They seemed, like himself, to be living in a world which did not want them. Why should he frighten them away? They took upon them more and more the aspect of gentle friends and pensioners – the only friends he could claim as being in the least degree interested in him, for his aunt had often told him that she was not. He ceased his rattling, and they alighted anew.

'Poor little dears!' said Jude, aloud. 'You *shall* have some dinner – you shall. There is enough for us all. Farmer Troutham can afford to let you have some. Eat, then, my dear little birdies, and make a good meal!'

They stayed and ate, inky spots on the nut-brown soil, and Jude enjoyed their appetite. A magic thread of fellow-feeling united his own life with theirs. Puny and sorry as those lives were, they much resembled his own.

(Part I, Chapter 2)

Hardy's earliest surviving poem, 'Domicilium', was written in his teens and lovingly depicts the cottage in which he was born and its natural setting. Formally, the poem shows the influence of Wordsworthian blank verse, and the impression given by this poem of a happy childhood spent with the natural world almost literally at the doorstep may also fairly be described as Wordsworthian. Such an outlook is, however, out of key with the attitudes reflected in Hardy's later work, and the difference may partly be ascribed to his reading of Darwin and other Victorian scientists, with their conception of a world in which the natural world is in truth in a constant state of warfare, each species preying upon others in the struggle for survival. By the time he wrote *Jude the Obscure*, nearly forty years after 'Domicilium', intellectual and personal factors had united to render his view of the world anything but Wordsworthian: a grim recognition of the brutal actualities had taken the place of an idealized and idyllic view of 'nature'.

In the passage quoted above, the hero and the narrator seem agreed in finding no beauty or charm in the English countryside: this is the kind of landscape – gently undulating arable land – that urban visitors might find appealing, but for Jude it is 'ugly' and for the narrator 'meanly utilitarian'. (This latter adjective implies that the field forms part of a farm run for profit.) The comparison of the field, with its pattern of parallel lines made by a horse-drawn harrow, to 'a piece of new corduroy' is certainly not one that would have ever occurred to Wordsworth, or to one of the more romantically minded nature poets of Hardy's own time: the comparison to a hard-wearing, factory-made material used for clothing worn by those engaged in manual labour seems indeed to expel any notion of the 'natural' as well as of the 'beautiful'.

In his own poetry, Hardy could view agricultural life romantically, as in a well-known poem, written at the time of the First World War, which opens as follows:

> Only a man harrowing clods
> In a slow silent walk
> With an old horse that stumbles and nods
> Half asleep as they stalk.
>
> ('In Time of "The Breaking of Nations"',
> 1915)

But in *Jude the Obscure* the view of the countryside, and of the lives of those who inhabit it, is altogether bleaker, and this is related to the

central fact that of all Hardy's novels this is the most uncompromisingly realistic. Twenty years earlier, in *Far from the Madding Crowd*, a
degree of idealization – for example, of the rural activities practised
by Gabriel Oak – had still been possible. Even in *Tess of the d'Urbervilles*, only a few years before *Jude*, the evocation of life in the Valley
of the Great Dairies is, as we have seen, highly romantic. In *Jude*,
however, Hardy – perhaps influenced by modern French realists such
as Gustave Flaubert and Emile Zola, as well as by the realist drama of
Henrik Ibsen, some of whose plays he had seen in London – seems
to be exploring a new kind of fiction that does not spare the reader
the harsh truth, however painful.

It is important to bear in mind that the narrator's role here is not
an entirely objective one: the impressions of the landscape that we
are given are filtered through the consciousness of a lonely and
unhappy child. Jude is an orphan, cared for by a great-aunt who
has no great aptitude or inclination for bringing up a small and
sensitive child, and the work he has to do – keeping the birds from
eating the corn, like a kind of diminutive human scarecrow – is, for
an intelligent lad who would like to be at school, stultifyingly monotonous. It also conflicts with his natural tenderness of heart (a quality
that is to prove a serious disadvantage to him in the aggressive and
competitive adult world he eventually enters): he cannot understand
why the birds should starve in order to make the prosperous farmer
still richer.

The young Jude's sense of emotional isolation, of finding himself in a world in which he has no rightful place, is reflected and
objectified in his physical situation. In the 'concave' field, he is alone
in a kind of bleak amphitheatre, the surrounding 'mist' helping to
create the illusion that this is the whole world – as, for the child, it for
the time being is. In the long paragraph beginning 'The fresh harrow-
lines . . .', Hardy is careful to point out that the apparent emptiness
of the scene is the result of Jude's ignorance of its role in
local history. Hardy is fascinated by 'texts' of all kinds that offer
themselves for scrutiny and interpretation: not only written
texts, ranging from books and letters to inscriptions painted on
a gate (as in *Tess*) or carved on a milestone (as later in *Jude*), but
non-verbal texts as diverse as a landscape and a human face.

In this instance, for anyone (like the narrator and Hardy himself) able to 'read' the landscape, it is full of interest, thanks to its association with past human lives and activities. But such a 'reading' is available only to those who have formed close associations with the spot over a long period, and Jude, who has not been born in the locality and does not really belong to it, is unskilled in this kind of 'reading'. Later he will endure difficulties and frustrations in learning to read the texts of ancient authors, but already he is unable to decipher the meaning of his surroundings, which themselves constitute a kind of ancient text. 'But this', as the narrator says, 'neither Jude nor the rooks around him considered' – and the linking of the boy and the birds prepares the reader for Jude's sympathy, expressed in both verbal and practical terms a little later, with the creatures who, like himself, are unwanted. (This point, at first implicit, is made explicit in the second sentence of the paragraph beginning 'He sounded the clacker...'.)

In this and many other respects, this scene from the protagonist's childhood touches on themes that will be developed at length in the novel. Jude's fundamental loneliness and sense of having no place in the world runs throughout the story, with its changing locations, until at the end Jude dies alone. His sense of being cut off from a communal and familial past makes him the most restless and no-madic of all Hardy's protagonists. When he tells the birds 'There is enough for us all,' he expresses the idealism which, like his sensitivity to the sufferings of others, is a grave handicap in a competitive modern society: 'enough for us all' – meaning that the farmer should reduce his profits in order to feed the hungry – is not a doctrine that would have commended itself to Victorian capitalism. The 'magic thread of fellow-feeling' makes Jude a finer human being than most of his contemporaries, but puts him at a disadvantage in a world in which he is already disadvantaged by his social background and his poverty.

'Nature' in this extract takes two forms, the living and the inanim-ate – more specifically, the birds (seen, in a sharply visual moment that is characteristically Hardyan, as 'inky spots on the nut-brown soil') and the landscape. The latter is indifferent to Jude's situation and feelings, and though its emptiness is more apparent than real (for to Hardy it is a text inscribed with innumerable histories), it is a world whose signs convey no meaning to the child. As for the birds, their lives 'much resembled' Jude's own, and in the next few paragraphs of Chapter 2 Jude finds himself punished and humiliated as a result of his instinctive feelings of goodwill towards these creatures. For Hardy, Nature, which treats wild creatures with what seems like wanton cruelty, sometimes extends the same treatment to humanity.

There is a sense, too, in which Jude's situation is defined in this passage in terms of negatives and absences. Earlier generations, fortified by an unquestioned Christian faith, might have seen the boy's fate as ordained by an inscrutable but all-wise Providence, and might have idealized or sentimentalized his work as bringing him into harmonious contact with the natural order. Hardy makes it perfectly clear, however, that Jude has no sense of belonging to any order at all. Physically he seems to be cut off from the rest of humankind, a small and solitary figure in the corn-field situated in a 'depression'. (Hardy probably intends no pun here, but there is a curious aptness in this word in relation to Jude's mental as well as his physical state.) 'The sky all round' is like a lid on a bowl that is, so to speak, sealed by the 'mist', and this heightens the claustrophobic sense of being enclosed and trapped. For a parallel in an earlier novel we may recall the scene at the Ring in *The Mayor of Casterbridge*, discussed above (p. 10). There, Michael Henchard, like Jude, was enclosed within an unbroken circle that seemed to limit his freedom of action.

Hardy's phrase 'the sky all round' calls for further comment. To a considerable extent the search for happiness in this novel, especially on the part of Jude and Sue, is conducted in terms of rival theologies or systems of faith, pagan and Christian. Both systems, however, share the concept of the sky or heaven as the abode of supernatural beings exerting an influence on human lives below. For Hardy, however, and the generation of those who have lost their faith for whom he speaks, the sky above Jude is empty and indifferent. An early poem of Hardy's is titled 'God's Funeral', and this conviction of the death of a God once believed to be all-powerful and all-loving creates a powerful and desolating sense of absence, here symbolized and objectified by the empty sky: the heavens are not open and limitless but, as already noted, enclosing like a cover on a bowl.

To the end of his long life Hardy never forgot the moment in childhood when his father placed into his hand a bird – a fieldfare – that had died of starvation in the harsh winter weather. This awareness of the bitter struggle for survival, intellectually confirmed and reinforced by his later reading of Darwin, informs his attitude to nature and makes it quite different from that of Wordsworth. In Chapter 3 of *Tess of the d'Urbervilles*, the narrator demands with irony, and even with scorn and bitterness, '...whence the poet whose philosophy is in these days deemed as profound and trustworthy as his song is breezy, gets his authority for speaking of "Nature's holy plan"'. Although Wordsworth is not actually named in this passage, the phrase is quoted from one of his *Lyrical Ballads*, and Hardy's scepticism towards such an optimistic and comforting view of nature is, if anything, even stronger in *Jude*.

Far from the Madding Crowd: Nature's Violence

Hardy had studied the Romantic poets very carefully but found himself, as we have seen, unable to accept Wordsworth's idea of nature as wise and benevolent, and as exercising a kind of parental role towards humanity. He often emphasizes the pain and suffering that observation and reflection revealed to him as part of the normal and inevitable order in the natural world. In the following passage the destructive power of a sudden change in the weather threatens to destroy the results of human labour.

> A light flapped over the scene, as if reflected from phosphorescent wings crossing the sky, and a rumble filled the air. It was the first move of the approaching storm.
>
> The second peal was noisy, with comparatively little visible lightning. Gabriel saw a candle shining in Bathsheba's bedroom, and soon a shadow swept to and fro upon the blind.
>
> Then there came a third flash. Manoeuvres of a most extraordinary kind were going on in the vast firmamental hollows overhead. The lightning now was the colour of silver, and gleamed in the heavens like a mailed army. Rumbles became rattles. Gabriel from his elevated

position could see over the landscape at least half-a-dozen miles in front. Every hedge, bush, and tree was distinct as in a line engraving. In a paddock in the same direction was a herd of heifers, and the forms of these were visible at this moment in the act of galloping about in the wildest and maddest confusion, flinging their heels and tails high into the air, their heads to earth. A poplar in the immediate foreground was like an ink stroke on burnished tin. Then the picture vanished, leaving the darkness so intense that Gabriel worked entirely by feeling with his hands.

He had stuck his ricking-rod, or poinard, as it was indifferently called – a long iron lance, polished by handling – into the stack, used to support the sheaves instead of the support called a groom used on houses. A blue light appeared in the zenith, and in some indescribable manner flickered down near the top of the rod. It was the fourth of the larger flashes. A moment later and there was a smack – smart, clear, and short. Gabriel felt his position to be anything but a safe one, and he resolved to descend.

Not a drop of rain had fallen as yet. He wiped his weary brow, and looked again at the black forms of the unprotected stacks. Was his life so valuable to him after all? What were his prospects that he should be so chary of running risk, when important and urgent labour could not be carried on without such risk? He resolved to stick to the stack. However, he took a precaution. Under the staddles was a long tethering chain, used to prevent the escape of errant horses. This he carried up the ladder, and sticking his rod through the clog at one end, allowed the other end of the chain to trail upon the ground. The spike attached to it he drove in. Under the shadow of this extemporized lightning-conductor he felt himself comparatively safe.

Before Oak had laid his hands upon his tools again out leapt the fifth flash, with the spring of a serpent and the shout of a fiend. It was green as an emerald, and the reverberation was stunning. What was this the light revealed to him? In the open ground before him, as he looked over the ridge of the rick, was a dark and apparently female form. Could it be that of the only venturesome woman in the parish – Bathsheba? The form moved on a step: then he could see no more.

'Is that you, ma'am?' said Gabriel to the darkness.

'Who is there?' said the voice of Bathsheba.

'Gabriel! I am on the rick, thatching.'

(Chapter 37)

Far from the Madding Crowd is often classified as a pastoral novel, though it would probably be just as accurate to describe it as anti-pastoral. It is true, however, that the community it depicts is a rural one in which most of the characters are engaged in various kinds of work on the land. Bathsheba's farm is the centre of the action, and though such characters as Sergeant Troy, Fanny Robin and Farmer Boldwood visit places outside this world, the farm and its immediate vicinity remains the focus of attention. In such circumstances, the natural world – including not only crops and sheep but seasonal changes and variations in weather conditions – has an immediate and significant effect on most of the human lives involved. In this scene, which forms the opening of Chapter 37, Gabriel struggles heroically, first alone, and then with Bathsheba's assistance, to save the ricks, which are threatened by an approaching storm that threatens to be severe and destructive.

In the previous chapter Gabriel has urged Troy to take action, but Troy has refused to do so. Moreover, he has encouraged the other farm-workers to drink too much, with the result that they are unable to lend a hand with this urgent task. The drama of the situation comes, therefore, from Gabriel's having to perform a difficult feat that would normally require a team of men to carry it out, and one in which every minute counts. It constitutes, in other words, a very familiar kind of fictional episode or crisis: the 'test' requiring exceptional powers to which a character is subjected, and through the performance of which his or her nature will be defined.

Hardy describes with systematic precision the various stages of 'the approaching storm'. It is an event that seems to dwarf humanity and human actions – a drama played out in 'the vast firmamental hollows overhead' (the word 'firmament', meaning sky or heavens, has Biblical overtones, occurring as it does in the Genesis account of the creation of the world). Hardy's description encourages the reader not just to conceptualize the storm but to hear and see it. The sounds of the thunder are carefully differentiated as first a 'rumble', then a 'peal', then 'a smack – smart, clear, and short'. And the visual aspect is, as so often in Hardy, sharply realized. He does not write vaguely about 'flashes of lightning', but differentiates between distinct kinds of natural phenomenon: the lightning is first 'the colour of silver', later 'green as an emerald'. Similes help us to relate these extraordinary manifestations to something more familiar and more easily grasped: there is an example in the opening sentence, and later the lightning is compared to 'a mailed army' and the scene is illuminated in sharp detail 'as in a line engraving'. That last phrase is particularly interesting, since Hardy is here relating his description of natural events to a branch of the visual arts. Elsewhere he states explicitly that 'the picture vanished': it is not just a scene but a *picture*, and it is in pictorial terms that Hardy has imagined and described it. (For some general comments on Hardy's pictorialism, see pp. 42–3 above.)

Taking the passage as a whole, however, it is possible to detect a balance between the portentously dramatic and the reassuringly familiar. The vast drama being played out in the skies makes 'a herd of heifers' go 'galloping about in the wildest and maddest confusion', and the reader is brought almost literally down to earth with the knowledgeable comment that such conditions have, among other things, an effect on farm animals. This detail points to a general characteristic of this novel, which sets a romantic story in a highly specific physical and social setting described with impressive authenticity.

The Mayor of Casterbridge: the Uncertainty of Harvests

The following passage has elements in common with the one just discussed, but introduces a new psychological element. Whereas the scene in *Far from the Madding Crowd* presented the struggle of a heroic individual with the forces of nature, we now find Michael Henchard engaged in a game of wits with the fluctuations of the weather and their economic implications. The weather will play a crucial role in the goodness or badness of the harvest that is just about to begin, and will therefore help to make or break Henchard's ailing commercial fortunes. What is now involved is not physical bravery but the inner resources of a man's nature in a situation that places him under great pressure, and the psychological drama of Henchard's vacillations between confidence and anxiety, and the mental struggle between reason and superstition, are key factors in the situation.

It was the eve of harvest. Prices being low Farfrae was buying. As was usual, after reckoning too surely on famine weather the local farmers had flown to the other extreme, and (in Farfrae's opinion) were selling off too recklessly – calculating with just a trifle too much certainty upon an abundant yield. So he went on buying old corn at its comparatively ridiculous price: for the produce of the previous year, though not large, had been of excellent quality.

When Henchard had squared his affairs in a disastrous way, and got rid of his burdensome purchases at a monstrous loss, the harvest began. There were three days of excellent weather, and then – 'What if that curst conjuror should be right after all!' said Henchard.

The fact was, that no sooner had the sickles begun to play than the atmosphere suddenly felt as if cress would grow in it without other nourishment. It rubbed people's cheeks like damp flannel when they walked abroad. There was a gusty, high, warm wind; isolated raindrops starred the window-panes at remote distances: the sunlight would flap out like a quickly opened fan, throw the pattern of the window upon the floor of the room in a milky, colourless shine, and withdraw as suddenly as it had appeared.

From that day and hour it was clear that there was not to be so successful an ingathering after all. If Henchard had only waited long enough he might at least have avoided loss though he had not made a profit. But the momentum of his character knew no patience. At this turn of the scales he remained silent. The movements of his mind seemed to tend to the thought that some power was working against him.

'I wonder,' he asked himself with eerie misgiving; 'I wonder if it can be that somebody has been roasting a waxen image of me, or stirring an unholy brew to confound me! I don't believe in such power; and yet – what if they should ha' been doing it!' Even he could not admit that the perpetrator, if any, might be Farfrae. These isolated hours of superstition came to Henchard in time of moody depression, when all his practical largeness of view had oozed out of him.

Meanwhile Donald Farfrae prospered. He had purchased in so depressed a market that the present moderate stiffness of prices was sufficient to pile for him a large heap of gold where a little one had been.

'Why, he'll soon be Mayor!' said Henchard. It was indeed hard that the speaker should, of all others, have to follow the triumphal chariot of this man to the Capitol.

The rivalry of the masters was taken up by the men.

September-night shades had fallen upon Casterbridge; the clocks had struck half-past eight, and the moon had risen. The streets of the town were curiously silent for such a comparatively early hour. A sound of jangling horse-bells and heavy wheels passed up the street. These were followed by angry voices outside Lucetta's house, which led her and Elizabeth-Jane to run to the windows, and pull up the blinds.

The neighbouring Market House and Town Hall abutted against its next neighbour the Church except in the lower storey, where an arched thoroughfare gave admittance to a large square called Bull Stake. A stone post rose in the midst, to which the oxen had formerly been tied for baiting with dogs to make them tender before they were killed in the adjoining shambles. In a corner stood the stocks.

The thoroughfare leading to this spot was now blocked by two four-horse waggons and horses, one laden with hay-trusses, the leaders having already passed each other, and become entangled head to tail. The passage of the vehicles might have been practicable if empty; but built up with hay to the bedroom windows as one way, it was impossible.

'You must have done it a' purpose!' said Farfrae's waggoner. 'You can hear my horses' bells half-a-mile such a night as this!'

'If ye'd been minding your business instead of zwailing along in such a gawk-hammer way, you would have zeed m'e!' retorted the wroth representative of Henchard.

(Chapter 27)

The passage occurs at the beginning of a chapter, and the first two sentences form an interesting conjunction. The expectations raised in the reader's mind by the phrase 'eve of harvest' are likely to be poetic and even sentimental: from Hardy, the established chronicler of rural life and work, we may expect to receive a description of communal labour by traditional methods, with a celebration of the earth's fertility. Such expectations are shattered, however, by the first word of the second sentence: 'Prices' places the emphasis firmly on the world of commerce, on agriculture as a business and a matter of financial profit and loss. In the same short sentence, the reference to Farfrae introduces one of the two key figures of the excerpt, for the central issue here will be the increasing rivalry between the younger man and the older one, Farfrae and Henchard, and the development of the pattern whereby the rise of the former is accompanied by the fall of the latter.

Farfrae's commercial shrewdness in buying good corn when it is being sold at a 'comparatively ridiculous price' is contrasted with the impulsiveness of the farmers, who respond 'too recklessly' to weather conditions that, as they should know from experience, may not continue. For, where the harvest is concerned, everything depends on the weather: fine or bad weather can make the difference between prosperity and ruin, or at least serious financial straits, and agriculture is dependent on unpredictable natural forces. In the previous chapter, Henchard has revealed the strong streak of superstition and irrationality in his character by visiting the 'conjuror' or weather-prophet, but is nevertheless wavering in his attitude towards the situation. His uncertainty and vacillation contrast strongly with the firmness and self-confidence shown by his rival.

In the third paragraph, Hardy invokes the atmospheric change, heralding a dramatic change in the weather, in a series of brilliantly vivid images. The writing here is poetic, even sensuous: we are not merely told that there is a rapid increase in humidity, but are stimulated to feel the change in the quality of the air, rubbing the cheeks 'like damp flannel'. The raindrops that 'starred' the windows (large drops splashing into a star-like pattern as they hit the glass), and the quality of the sunlight ('a milky, colourless shine'), are visually precise, while the choice of words is sometimes unexpected and poetic ('flap out', as a description of the sudden, brief appearance of the sun's rays).

The fourth paragraph, however, turns from the external and visible world to the psychology of the protagonist. It becomes clear that Henchard is not only heading for ruin but doing so in a dogged, wilful, almost self-destructive way. The alternative road is indicated ('If Henchard had only waited long enough...'), but, given his impulsive nature, it is not a road he is capable of taking. For 'the momentum of his character knew no patience'. The narrator makes it clear that this moment represents a 'turn of the scales' in Henchard's fortunes and destiny. And the concluding reference to his sense of 'some power...working against him' again underlines his superstitious nature: Farfrae would never have entertained such a thought. In psychoanalytic terms, it may perhaps be interpreted as originating in Henchard's sense of guilt and his awareness that he deserves to be punished for his conduct at the beginning of the novel. This is not, however, an interpretation of the situation that would have occurred to Henchard (or perhaps to many others in that pre-Freudian age), and he entertains the idea that some enemy has been practising black magic against him ('roasting a waxen image of me').

Farfrae, in contrast, has taken advantage of the uncertainty and vacillation of other dealers, and is prospering. This leads Henchard to reflect that, as things are going, Farfrae is likely to succeed him as Mayor. This insight in fact points forward to subsequent developments in the story, and it would not be much of an exaggeration to say that the future development of the story is largely implied in this passage, occurring little more than halfway through the novel. This is evidence of the strong construction of *The Mayor of Casterbridge*, which, though a fairly long and action-filled work, essentially represents a development of the 'life and death' formula announced in the full title.

The last part of the excerpt turns from description and comment to a dramatic incident that illustrates the generalization that 'The rivalry of the masters was taken up by the men.' At this stage there has been no open conflict between Henchard and Farfrae, but the collision of the vehicles and the angry exchanges of the men externalize the hidden feelings of aggression that are already in existence on Henchard's side. For he and Farfrae may also be said to be on a collision course, and later the two of them will engage in actual physical struggle. At the same time, the lively dialogue, with its use of dialect ('zwailing', 'gawk-hammer') and non-standard pronunciations and grammatical forms ('a' purpose' for 'on purpose', 'zeed' for 'saw'), offers stylistic contrast with the formal language of the narrative voice.

Conclusions

The four passages exemplify radically varying attitudes to nature. The idyllic phase spent by Tess at the Talbothays dairy-farm has many of the attributes of traditional pastoral, a literary convention that dates back to the ancient world: isolated from the pressures of the modern world in this rural backwater, Tess and Angel are free to fall in love in a setting, and at a season, that seem to harmonize with their happiness. It must be said, though, that there is a characteristically Hardyan emphasis on the role of *work*, since the lovers are not simply playing a romantic game (as often in traditional pastoral) but are both employed in useful labour. It is, however, a form of labour that pre-dates the Industrial Revolution, and indeed the lovers seem for a time to stand outside history. All too soon, the idyll will come to an end, and the hardships Tess undergoes at Flintcomb-Ash represent a kind of anti-pastoral that forms a bold contrast with the Talbothays scenes.

There is no harmony between humanity and nature in the scene in which the young Jude becomes aware of his own isolation and alienation. What is implied in this picture of rural life is a Darwinian struggle for existence, in which the power and ingenuity of humanity can only cause suffering and death to wild creatures. Jude's pity for the birds makes him a sympathetic character, but the reader also becomes aware that his sense of pain at their sufferings will be a handicap to him in a world in which he too will have to take part in the struggle for survival.

Nature, then, can also seem hostile, or at best indifferent, to human endeavours. Its capacity for violence and destructiveness is evident in Gabriel's Oak's struggle to protect the products of hard work in the fields from the approaching storm. As well as invoking the power of natural forces, the passage from *Far from the Madding Crowd* reinforces the reader's sense of Gabriel's quiet heroism. In *The Mayor of Casterbridge* a change in the weather also provides a testing situation, but it is one in which the protagonist in this case, Michael Henchard, fails to rise to the occasion. The uncertainty whether the harvest will be a good one or not elicits from him a range of reactions that include rashness, superstition and depression. The psychological element is much stronger and more complex in this passage than in the one from the earlier novel.

More generally speaking, 'nature' remains a highly complex concept and a word that has undergone significant shifts of meaning over the centuries, mirroring profound changes not only in taste and modes of perception but in religious and philosophical ideas. It is proper to ask, therefore, to what extent Hardy's presentation of nature embodies his views on the universe. For Hardy, too, it is a multilayered rather than a simple concept. At the most obvious level 'nature' can refer to the non-human world of landscape, vegetation and animal life that we have in mind when we speak of 'the beauty of nature' (this begs for a moment the interesting question of how far the English countryside as Hardy knew it was a product of human intervention). Hardy's prose and verse are full of detailed and richly informed accounts of this world seen under the aspects of the varying seasons, and such depictions often incorporate a strong element of realism or naturalism.

In these terms nature lies outside humanity and is often implicitly or explicitly set in contrast with human elements and human creations such as towns, cities and institutions. Nature can be exploited or abused as well as respected, valued and enjoyed, and Hardy does not shrink from presenting the uglier side of the human impact on the natural world, as when Tess discovers the dying pheasants, or Jude is disturbed by the agonized cries of a rabbit caught in a trap. More broadly, the highlighting of urban communities in *Jude* at the end of Hardy's novel-writing career represents a recognition that the natural environment is seriously threatened by the profound social and economic changes that took place in nineteenth-century England. To a less prominent extent, the course of Tess's short life takes her from small rural communities 'close to nature' to the fashionable and rapidly growing town of Sandbourne (Bournemouth) and the administrative centre of Wintoncester (Winchester).

Hardy also makes no secret of the fact that the natural world itself, rightly understood, is no pastoral idyll but is engaged in a perpetual state of bloody warfare. There exists an endless struggle for existence in which every species is either predator or victim, and individual members of a species are involved in a fiercely competitive fight to survive at the expense, if necessary, of their fellows. Just as humanity, in its cruelty to animals or its indifference to their sufferings, takes its place among the ruthless predators, so humans prey on each other and the struggle for existence has its counterpart in human lives. Fine and gentle natures like Tess Durbeyfield and Jude Fawley are ill-equipped for success in the battle of life and succumb in the face of competition from, or exploitation by, the stronger members of their species.

Already, it should be noted, we have moved from a simple and external view of nature to a sense of nature as embodying a world-view. Although there are strong realistic and naturalistic elements in Hardy's fiction, his presentation of nature often seems to be a means of making a philosophical or ethical statement. In his fiction he is less concerned with presenting a 'picture' of the external world (as he might do, and often does, in a short lyric poem) as with presenting suggestive symbols that invite the reader to ponder their deeper meanings. Thus the storm against which Gabriel Oak contends (and Troy declines to contend) is not just a meteorological phenom-enon but a force that seems almost endowed with will and purpose, and the same is true of the seemingly capricious changes in the weather that help to ruin Henchard's fortunes.

Another good example of this occurs in Chapter 43 of *Tess*. In obvious ways the barren upland farm at Flintcomb-Ash stands in severe realistic contrast to the poetic and idyllic Talbothays phase of Tess's life. In the passage beginning 'There had not been such a winter for years . . .', the external manifestations of the bitter weather are invoked in detail. But this harshness is also an externalization of the heroine's inner state after her rejection by her husband, and Hardy soon turns from a kind of word-painting to the introduction of a powerful and disturbing symbol that might have come out of a Romantic poem such as Coleridge's *Rime of the Ancient Mariner*: 'strange birds from beyond the North Pole began to arrive silently . . .'. Though silent, these creatures bring their own message, for they are 'gaunt spectral creatures with tragical eyes – eyes which had witnessed scenes of cataclysmal horror in inaccessible polar regions of a magnitude such as no human being had ever con-ceived . . .'. Their message, it seems, is of a universe capable of unimaginable horror and tragedy, and one in which Tess's personal tragedy seems inevitable and almost 'natural'.

It was an audacious stroke on Hardy's part to introduce these strange birds (one of a series of bird-references in this novel) into the familiar region of Wessex. On a realistic level he is justified by the exceptional weather conditions, but the birds are undoubtedly more than a picturesque addition to the realistic description. They have a haunting symbolic power that goes beyond their immediate signifi- cance, and it is interesting that Hardy should have introduced a similar image into one of his finest poems, the richly symbolic 'During Wind and Rain', where 'the white storm-birds wing across'. In the fiction such symbols often possess an element of the bizarre, the non-naturalistic, even the grotesque – or, to use one of Hardy's own favourite words in speaking of his own art, the idiosyncratic.

For Hardy, then, nature can have many meanings. It can denote the external non-human world available for our aesthetic apprecia- tion and enjoyment. It can be one of the terms in a dualistic view that contrasts the natural with the products of human intervention. It can embody a philosophical view of existence that owes much to nine- teenth-century science in general and Darwinian ideas of evolution in particular. And it can also be a source of poetic symbols that suggest meanings not readily communicated through the tradition of fictional realism in which Hardy largely but by no means exclusively worked.

Methods of Analysis

The main concern in these passages is the relationship between the human and the non-human world, and the presentation of the latter has involved Hardy in a considerable amount of description – of scenery, animals and birds, the season and the weather. Our analysis has therefore necessarily focussed to a large extent upon descriptive elements. Descriptive prose is one of the components in a work of fiction that runs alongside such other elements as narrative, dialogue and commentary to create a complex experience for the reader – to create a fictional 'world' that bears a relationship to the world we know or know about. Hardy's descriptive writing is often precise and detailed, inspiring confidence in his knowledge of the material described: the urban reader, for example, would learn something about dairy-farming from the Talbothays scenes in *Tess*, as well as about the landscape and land-use of Wessex. At the same time this realism is complemented by poetic, even sensuous writing that is often strongly visual (consider, for instance, the description of the sudden atmospheric change, in the extract from *The Mayor of Casterbridge*).

Suggestions for Further Work

Of the four novels under discussion, the richest in their descriptions of the natural world and rural activities are *Far from the Madding Crowd* and *Tess of the d'Urbervilles*; in their different ways, the other two novels place more emphasis on urban life. You may like to look closely at the second chapter of *Far from the Madding Crowd*, from the beginning to ' "One o'clock," said Gabriel'; also at the account of Tess's labours at Flintcomb-Ash in *Tess of the d'Urbervilles*, Chapter 43, from the beginning to 'from the spirits'.

4

Individuals and Communities

Introduction

Most of Hardy's novels embody a strong sense of community – the outstanding exception, as we shall see, is his last, *Jude the Obscure* – but the characters typically include both insiders and outsiders. At the most obvious level, Hardy's characters may be divided into those who belong to a community by virtue of birth and upbringing (with all that these imply in terms of knowledge and loyalty), and those who are interlopers or strangers from elsewhere. In *Tess*, for instance, there is a profound gulf between the heroine and her family, who have for generations been established residents of Marlott, and the *nouveau riche* family to which Alec belongs and which has only recently settled there with the aim of winning a place in the social hierarchy of the district. In *Far from the Madding Crowd*, though Sergeant Troy belongs to a local family, he has chosen to spend his life elsewhere. As a professional soldier, Troy has embraced a career that involves mobility, and has no particular affiliation – as Gabriel Oak, for instance, emphatically has – with the rural world of which he becomes a member through his marriage to Bathsheba.

On a somewhat subtler level, there are more sympathetic characters, like Tess herself and like Michael Henchard in *The Mayor of Casterbridge*, who are both insiders and outsiders. Tess in particular begins as a member of a community that subsequently rejects her and sends her on a series of wanderings that end only in her death. But even earlier her schooling has created a gap between herself and the other village girls, so that she hovers uneasily between two social classes and two cultural traditions (see the quotation on p. 182 below). Henchard begins as an outsider newly arrived in Caster-bridge, wins a leading place in the community, but is later rejected and goes into voluntary exile.

Another aspect of Hardy's depiction of the community is his account of it, in nearly every one of his novels, as under threat and even in process of disintegration. Ancient customs like the shearing supper in *Far from the Madding Crowd*, the skimmington ride in *The Mayor*, and the club-walking at the beginning of *Tess* are like threatened species, in process of being overtaken by a world that has changed so rapidly that they cannot much longer find a place. This process becomes most obvious in *Jude the Obscure*: see, for example, the reference to the rebuilt church at the end of the first chapter (discussed below, p. 116), and to the allusions throughout that novel to the system of railways that had transformed the patterns and rhythms of life in Britain during the nineteenth century.

Far from the Madding Crowd: 'in harmony'

Considered chronologically, Hardy's novels move from the depiction of a small and often isolated community in which individuals have an acknowledged and long-established place, to the portrayal of a rapidly changing society characterized by restlessness and mobility. We shall see later in this chapter that in his novels of the 1880s and 1890s Hardy dramatizes the plight of those who, for one reason or another, no longer occupy a secure and well-defined place in relation to the community. But in the relatively early *Far from the Madding Crowd*, life and work for most of the characters embody continuity and tradition. In the rural community of Weatherbury, the building that most strikingly symbolizes this is the great barn, the central subject of the following passage:

It was the first day of June, and the sheep-shearing season culminated, the landscape, even to the leanest pasture, being all health and colour. Every green was young, every pore was open, and every stalk was swollen with racing currents of juice. God was palpably present in the country, and the devil had gone with the world to town. Flossy catkins of the later kinds, ferny sprouts like bishops' croziers, the square-headed moschatel, the odd cuckoo-pint – like an apoplectic saint in a niche of malachite, – snow-white ladies'-smocks, the toothwort, approximating to human flesh, the enchanter's night-shade, and the black-petalled doleful-bells, were among the quainter objects of the vegetable world in and about Weatherbury at this teeming time; and of the animal, the metamorphosed figures of Mr Jan Coggan, the master-shearer; the second and third shearers, who travelled in the exercise of their calling, and do not require definition by name; and Henery Fray the fourth shearer, Susan Tall's husband the fifth, Joseph Poorgrass the sixth, young Cain Ball as assistant shearer, and Gabriel Oak as general supervisor. None of these were clothed to any extent worth mentioning, each appearing to have hit in the matter of raiment the decent mean between a high and low caste Hindoo. An angularity of lineament, and a fixity of facial machinery in general, proclaimed that serious work was the order of the day.

They sheared in the great barn, called for the nonce the Shearing-barn, which on ground-plan resembled a church with transepts. It not only emulated the form of the neighbouring church of the parish, but vied with it in antiquity. Whether the barn had ever formed one of a group of conventual buildings nobody seemed to be aware; no trace of such surroundings remained. The vast porches at the sides, lofty enough to admit a waggon laden to its highest with corn in the sheaf, were spanned by heavy-pointed arches of stone, broadly and boldly cut, whose very simplicity was the origin of a grandeur not apparent in erections where more ornament has been attempted. The dusky, filmed, chestnut roof, braced and tied in by huge collars, curves, and diagonals, was far nobler in design, because more wealthy in material, than nine-tenths of those in our modern churches. Along each side wall was a range of striding buttresses, throwing deep shadows on the spaces between them, which were perforated by lancet openings, combining in their proportions the precise requirements both of beauty and ventilation.

One could say about this barn, what could hardly be said of either the church or the castle, akin to it in age and style, that the purpose which had dictated its original erection was the same with that to which it was still applied. Unlike and superior to either of those two typical remnants of mediaevalism, the old barn embodied practices which had suffered no mutilation at the hands of time. Here at least the spirit of the ancient builders was at one with the spirit of the modern beholder. Standing before this abraded pile, the eye regarded its present usage, the mind dwelt upon its past history, with a satisfied sense of functional continuity throughout – a feeling almost of gratitude, and quite of pride, at the permanence of the idea which had heaped it up. The fact that four centuries had neither proved it to be founded on a mistake, inspired any hatred of its purpose, nor given rise to any reaction that had battered it down, invested this simple grey effort of old minds with a repose, if not a grandeur, which a too curious reflection was apt to disturb in its ecclesiastical and military compeers. For once mediaevalism and modernism had a common standpoint. The lanceolate windows, the time-eaten arch-stones and chamfers, the orientation of the axis, the misty chestnut work of the rafters, referred to no exploded fortifying art or worn-out religious creed. The defence and salvation of the body by daily bread is still a study, a religion, and a desire.

Today the large side doors were thrown open towards the sun to admit a bountiful light to the immediate spot of the shearers' operations, which was the wood threshing-floor in the centre, formed of thick oak, black with age and polished by the beating of flails for many generations, till it had grown as slippery and as rich in hue as the state-room floors of an Elizabethan mansion. Here the shearers knelt, the sun slanting in upon their bleached shirts, tanned arms, and the polished shears they flourished, causing these to bristle with a thousand rays strong enough to blind a weak-eyed man. Beneath them a captive sheep lay panting, quickening its pants as misgiving merged in terror, till it quivered like the hot landscape outside.

This picture of today in a frame of four hundred years ago did not produce that marked contrast between ancient and modern which is implied by the contrast of date. In comparison with cities, Weatherbury was immutable. The citizen's *Then* is the rustic's *Now*. In London, twenty or thirty years ago are old times; in Paris ten years, or five; in Weatherbury three or four score years were included in the mere present, and nothing less than a century set a mark on its face or tone. Five decades hardly modified the cut of a gaiter, the embroidery of a smock-frock, by the breadth of a hair. Ten generations failed to alter the turn of a single phrase. In these Wessex nooks the busy outsider's ancient times are only old; his old times are still new; his present is futurity.

So the barn was natural to the shearers, and the shearers were in harmony with the barn.

(Chapter 22)

Unlike most of the passages examined in this book, the above is entirely undramatic, containing no action or dialogue: the mode throughout is of narratorial description and commentary. The ostensible subject is an ancient building, the great barn at Weatherbury, but this is used as a starting-point for essayistic reflections on history and architecture, city and countryside, work, religion, and other topics. At the same time the barn and the way of life it represents has a close connection with the character and values of the novel's hero, Gabriel Oak.

At this point in the novel, the barn is the scene of a specific activity that has to be performed every year at the appropriate season and has thus been performed since time immemorial. That activity is sheep-shearing. Hardy is well aware that this is an extremely ancient activity, and that the nineteenth-century workers are engaged in very similar labour to that undertaken by their distant predecessors who tended the flocks of the Old Testament patriarchs such as Abraham and Jacob. (The last sentence of the extract quoted, with its archaic pattern of syntax ('So... and...'), its repetitions and its balance between the two parts, has a strongly Biblical flavour that can hardly have been accidental.)

The barn thus represents the age-old human engagement in labour designed to sustain life, and in this respect it is contrasted with the two other important buildings of the neighbourhood, the church and the castle. All three date from about the same period, the later Middle Ages, but (Hardy suggests) only the barn has retained its validity and has a place in modern life. The law and order of modern society have made redundant the castle as a heavily defended stronghold; the decline of faith is making the church equally redundant. (Here Hardy anticipates a well-known modern poem, Philip Larkin's 'Church Going', and it is probably relevant that as a poet Larkin was deeply influenced by Hardy.) But the importance of the barn, and its centrality to the life of the community, survive, and it represents an unbroken continuity between past and present. Hardy both prized such continuities and persistently lamented their disappearance.

The passage begins by establishing the time of year and the seasonal context. It is a period of intense growth and fertility in the natural world and the rural scene – 'all health and colour' in 'this teeming time'. The precise cataloguing of wild flowers, with their traditional country names and their attributes indicated, leaves us in no doubt that the writer is intimately familiar with and knowledgeable concerning such scenes. Much more familiar, in all probability, than most of his readers, who would have belonged to the 'town' to which the devil, it is mischievously suggested, has transferred himself. (The sentence in question seems to incorporate a buried allusion to a famous line by the eighteenth-century poet William Cowper, 'God made the country, and Man made the town'.)

From 'the vegetable world', attention is transferred to the 'animal' and specifically the human, as the group of sheep-shearers is introduced. This is a team which must work together and in which every member has a part to play, but there is a clear and unquestioned hierarchy with Gabriel Oak, the novel's hero, at the top. The narrator's stance at this point seems to have undergone a shift: it is now very much that of an outsider – of one who under no circumstances would himself play a part in such an activity – and the dress and facial expressions of the men are described with a rather heavy-handed facetiousness that may even seem a little patronizing. At such moments Hardy seems to be sitting rather uneasily on the fence. He is prepared to write in an informed and even an affectionate and committed way about country life, but he does not wish to be supposed to be a countryman: his preferred role is, indeed, that of metropolitan man of letters. But it would be obvious to most readers that a man who could write in this way must have a close knowledge of rural matters, and some contemporary critics were in their turn prepared to patronize Hardy.

The subsequent paragraphs deal with the barn itself, and in describing its physical structure Hardy draws on his long training and experience as an architect. In writing of the design and materials, he draws on the technical vocabulary of the architect ('lanceolate windows', 'arch-stones and chamfers'), and when, for instance, he describes the interior of the roof, he does so with an expert knowledge of the kind of wood that has been used and how it is held in place, as well as a sensuous and aesthetic appreciation of its appearance: 'the dusky, filmed, chestnut roof, braced and tied in by huge collars, curves, and diagonals...'.

The barn, then, is a physical reality evoked by Hardy in precise detail. But it is also a symbol of, as he puts it, 'functional continuity': that is, it still serves the purpose for which it was originally constructed. And this can be said of neither the castle nor the church, which are ancient monuments rather than buildings with a valid place in modern life. In his comments on the church having outlived its original purpose, surviving from an age of faith into an age of doubt and unbelief, we encounter an apparent paradox in Hardy's thinking. His praise for the barn and all it stands for suggests a conservative and traditionalist standpoint, but the comments on the church seem radical, sceptical, subversive.

Can this paradox be explained? One explanation may be that, whereas the Anglican church has often been associated with the upper and middle classes, the barn is the centre of the labours of working men. And though Hardy's life and career were a case-study in upward mobility, his deepest affiliations were with the class into which he was born and in which his early and formative years were spent. Historically, too, the church in the Victorian period was losing its hold on the rapidly urbanized population at the same time as being split by internal disputes; the barn, on the other hand, retained a central place in the life of the community, and was likely to do so as long as people needed food and clothing.

The final section of the passage broadens the context in order to offer some comparative reflections on rural and urban life, and in particular on attitudes to history, time and change. In areas of life such as dress and speech, the rapid changes or shifts of fashion that characterize city life have no counterpart in the country, where change comes much more slowly. The phrase 'Wessex nooks' is significant: the novels are set in localities that lie, as Hardy puts it in another novel, 'outside the gates of the world'. (The word 'Wessex', formerly used mainly by historians to denote the old Saxon kingdom, was revived by Hardy in *Far from the Madding Crowd* and used by him throughout his later work to refer to the half-real, half-fictitious settings of his fiction.)

These rural 'nooks', too, will eventually be overtaken by change and 'progress', but for the time being the traditional ways of life and work continue, and the barn symbolizes this inherited system of customs and values. The 'harmony' between the workers and their setting has been produced by time and tradition, and has no counter-part (it is implied) in the new urban communities that were one of the most remarkable creations of the nineteenth century.

Tess of the d'Urbervilles: the 'club-walking'

The following excerpt, from very near the beginning of the novel, introduces Tess as a member of a social group. She is one of a number of mostly young women who are participating in a traditional annual ceremony still precariously surviving. But just as the tradition is itself threatened by change, there are already ominous hints that Tess's fate may turn out to be different from that of the other 'genuine country girls' with whom she seems at present to be on an equal footing.

> The district is of historic, no less than of topographical interest. The Vale was known in former times as the Forest of White Hart, from a curious legend of King Henry III's reign, in which the killing by a certain Thomas de la Lynd of a beautiful white hart which the king had run down and spared, was made the occasion of a heavy fine. In those days, and till comparatively recent times, the country was densely wooded. Even now, traces of its earlier condition are to be found in the old oak copses and irregular belts of timber that yet survive upon its slopes, and the hollow-trunked trees that shade so many of its pastures.
>
> The forests have departed, but some old customs of their shades remain. Many, however, linger only in a metamorphosed or disguised form. The May-Day dance, for instance, was to be discerned on the afternoon under notice, in the guise of the club revel, or 'club-walking', as it was there called.

It was an interesting event to the younger inhabitants of Marlott, though its real interest was not observed by the participators in the ceremony. Its singularity lay less in the retention of a custom of walking in procession and dancing on each anniversary than in the members being solely women. In men's clubs such celebrations were, though expiring, less uncommon; but either the natural shyness of the softer sex, or a sarcastic attitude on the part of male relatives, had denuded such women's clubs as remained (if any other did) of this their glory and consummation. The club of Marlott alone lived to uphold the local Cerealia. It had walked for hundreds of years, if not as benefit-club, as votive sisterhood of some sort; and it walked still.

The banded ones were all dressed in white gowns – a gay survival from Old Style days, when cheerfulness and May-time were synonyms – days before the habit of taking long views had reduced emotions to a monotonous average. Their first exhibition of themselves was in a processional march of two and two round the parish. Ideal and real clashed slightly as the sun lit up their figures against the green hedges and creeper-laced house-fronts; for though the whole troop wore white garments, no two whites were alike among them. Some approached pure blanching; some had a bluish pallor; some worn by the older characters (which had possibly lain by folded for many a year) inclined to a cadaverous tint, and to a Georgian style.

In addition to the distinction of a white frock, every woman and girl carried in her right hand a peeled willow wand, and in her left a bunch of white flowers. The peeling of the former, and the selection of the latter, had been an operation of personal care.

There were a few middle-aged and even elderly women in the train, their silver-wiry hair and wrinkled faces, scourged by time and trouble, having almost a grotesque, certainly a pathetic, appearance in such a jaunty situation. In a true view, perhaps, there was more to be gathered and told of each anxious and experienced one, to whom the years were drawing nigh when she should say, 'I have no pleasure in them', than of her juvenile comrades. But let the elder be passed over here for those under whose bodices the life throbbed quick and warm.

The young girls formed, indeed, the majority of the band, and their heads of luxurious hair reflected in the sunshine every one of gold, and black, and brown. Some had beautiful eyes, others a beautiful nose, others a beautiful mouth and figure: few, if any, had all. A difficulty of arranging their lips in this crude exposure to public scrutiny, an inability to balance their heads, and to dissociate self-consciousness from their features, was apparent in them, and showed that they were genuine country girls, unaccustomed to many eyes.

And as each and all of them were warmed without by the sun, so each had a private little sun for her soul to bask in; some dream, some affection, some hobby, at least some remote and distant hope which, though perhaps starving to nothing, still lived on, as hopes will. Thus they were all cheerful, and many of them merry.

They came round by The Pure Drop Inn, and were turning out of the high road to pass through a wicket-gate into the meadows, when one of the women said –

'The Lord-a-Lord! Why, Tess Durbeyfield, if there isn't thy father riding hwome in a carriage!'

A young member of the band turned her head at the exclamation. She was a fine and handsome girl – not handsomer than some others, possibly – but her mobile peony mouth and large innocent eyes added eloquence to colour and shape. She wore a red ribbon in her hair, and was the only one of the white company who could boast of such a pronounced adornment.

(Chapter 2)

Hardy's method in this passage is to start from the broad historical and social context of the scene and then to move through a series of increasingly detailed close-ups to the figure of Tess, who here appears for the first time. At the beginning of the first paragraph, the word 'historic' strikes a keynote, and the following lines describe changes in the Wessex landscape over a long period of time: no more than 'traces of its earlier condition' now remain in an area once covered by forest. This point forms a bridge into the next paragraph, which begins 'The forests have departed' and goes on to show that human activities, including 'old customs', are in the process of suffering the same fate as the landscape. Many customs have disappeared without trace along with the forests; those that have survived do so only in 'a metamorphosed or disguised form'. Here, as so often in Hardy, Darwinian ideas of the struggle for survival (and failure to survive) and of change and adaptation are applied not only to the biological world but to human society.

These opening paragraphs thus demonstrate that, with the passing of time, both the physical and social worlds have been changed almost beyond recognition. The focus then narrows as Hardy directs the reader's attention to a particular ancient custom, the club revel or club-walking, which involved a May-time procession around the village. Though this was formerly carried out by both men and women, the latter still keep up the tradition in one place only – the village of Marlott, where Tess has her home. The appurtenances of the ceremony are unchanged – the white gowns, the 'peeled willow wand' carried in one hand and the 'bunch of white flowers' in the other – but it is suggested that the original significance of the custom has been forgotten and the ceremony is carried out only from habit and for sentimental or nostalgic reasons. It is also implied, perhaps, that even in Marlott the tradition is not likely to last much longer: the tide of change, which has swept it away in all other communities, will do the same in Marlott.

When it comes to the original significance of this custom, Hardy has to tread carefully. For the custom in question was fairly obviously a fertility ritual, and the willow wands probably phallic symbols. (The pagan origins are perhaps hinted at in the narrator's slightly pedantic allusion to 'the local Cerealia': in ancient Rome, the Cerealia was a festival held in honour of Ceres, goddess of crops and fertility, whose name is the origin of our own word 'cereal'.) What is fairly obvious to the modern reader, however, would not have been obvious to all Victorian readers, and considerations of propriety, enforced by editors and publishers as well as by the reactions of readers, would not have permitted the writer of mass-readership fiction to explain and elaborate such points. The sexual origins and associations of the custom are, however, highly relevant to the fictional situation, since Tess is depicted from the outset in a sexual context, and even as a victim. Those white gowns symbolize virginal purity, a quality that in Tess's case is soon to be lost as a result of her encounter with Alec.

A further and related symbolic touch is the 'red ribbon' that Tess wears in her hair. She is the only girl to do so, and this has the effect of isolating her from the group to which, in other respects, she appears to belong. This vivid visual detail forms a very early hint of a point that will be extensively developed later. In some ways a typical village girl, Tess is also distinguished from her peers in a variety of ways, including her ancient family (and family name) and her superior education. She both belongs and does not belong, is typical and untypical, and from this ambivalence spring difficulties and eventually tragedy.

The red ribbon is also the first of a series of allusions in this novel to the colour red, particularly in contrast with white, that are associated with Tess at various stages of Tess's story. This pattern of colour-symbolism culminates in the red spot on the white ceiling after the murder of Alec. It may be said that Tess is associated with the idea of blood from a very early stage of her history.

Another symbolic detail occurs near the beginning of the passage, in the reference to 'the Forest of White Hart'. A hart is a male deer, in former times pursued and killed for sport as well as food, especially by the upper classes. Tess, too, will become a 'white' or virginal victim of the (spuriously) upper-class Alec, and this again is part of a pattern of allusions – in this case, allusions that compare Tess to, or associate her with, some shy and vulnerable wild creature. In the very last paragraph of the novel, the idea of a helpless victim of 'sport' recurs in the much-discussed reference to the 'President of the Immortals' having 'ended his sport with Tess'. Such patterns of recurring metaphor and symbol remind us that Hardy, who at times seems to be writing like a historian or chronicler of rural England, is simultaneously constructing a poetic kind of novel in which recurring imagery plays a role comparable to that in Shakespearean drama.

The overall effect of the passage, reflected in its structure, is to place Tess in the context of a community. From the historical setting, attention moves to the survival of ancient customs, then to the representatives of these ceremonies viewed collectively. Finally, the snatch of dialogue referring to Tess's father both links the scene with what has happened in the opening chapter and introduces Tess herself – still a member of the group, but already marked out, visually and symbolically, as one different from the rest, and implicitly reserved for a different fate. Much of what follows in the rest of the novel represents a development of points hinted at in this early passage.

Jude the Obscure: the Outsider

Unlike Tess, Jude has never really belonged to a community. An orphan, he has left his birthplace to live with an unmarried great-aunt who somewhat grudgingly brings him up. Later, the failure of his marriage to Arabella and his ambitions to become a scholar lead him to leave the district and begin the series of wanderings that end only with his death. In the following extract he is shown to be in Christminster but not of it: Jude's display of learning takes place not in a college but in a low-class pub and before an ignorant audience. Christminster contains two different communities, 'town' and 'gown' – the city and the university – and both are represented in the pub. But Jude belongs to neither.

> Jude Fawley, with the self-conceit, effrontery, and *aplomb* of a strong-brained fellow in liquor, threw in his remarks somewhat peremptorily; and his aims having been what they were for so many years, everything the others said turned upon his tongue, by a sort of mechanical craze, to the subject of scholarship and study, the extent of his own learning being dwelt upon with an insistence that would have appeared pitiable to himself in his sane hours.
>
> 'I don't care a damn,' he was saying, 'for any Provost, Warden, Principal, Fellow, or cursed Master of Arts in the University! What I know is that I'd lick 'em on their own ground if they'd give me a chance, and show 'em a few things they are not up to yet!'
>
> 'Hear, hear!' said the undergraduates from the corner, where they were talking privately about the pups.
>
> 'You always was fond o' books, I've heard,' said Tinker Taylor, 'and I don't doubt what you state. Now with me 'twas different. I always saw there was more to be learnt outside a book than in; and I took my steps accordingly, or I shouldn't have been the man I am.'
>
> 'You aim at the Church, I believe?' said Uncle Joe. 'If you are such a scholar as to pitch yer hopes so high as that, why not give us a specimen of your scholarship? Canst say the Creed in Latin, man? That was how they once put it to a chap down in my country.'
>
> 'I should think so!' said Jude haughtily.
>
> 'Not he! Like his conceit!' screamed one of the ladies.
>
> 'Just you shut up, Bower o'Bliss!' said one of the undergraduates. 'Silence!' He drank off the spirits in his tumbler, rapped with it on the

counter, and announced, 'The gentleman in the corner is going to rehearse the Articles of his Belief, in the Latin tongue, for the edification of the company.'

'I won't!' said Jude.

'Yes – have a try!' said the surplice-maker.

'You can't!' said Uncle Joe.

'Yes, he can!' said Tinker Taylor.

'I'll swear I can!' said Jude. 'Well, come now, stand me a small Scotch cold, and I'll do it straight off.'

'That's a fair offer,' said the undergraduate, throwing down the money for the whisky.

The barmaid concocted the mixture with the bearing of a person compelled to live amongst animals of an inferior species, and the glass was handed across to Jude, who, having drunk the contents, stood up and began rhetorically, without hesitation:

'*Credo in unum Deum, Patrem omnipotentem, Factorem coeli et terrae, visibilium omnium et invisibilium.*'

'Good! Excellent Latin!' cried one of the undergraduates, who, however, had not the slightest conception of a single word.

A silence reigned among the rest in the bar, and the maid stood still, Jude's voice echoing sonorously into the inner parlour, where the landlord was dozing, and bringing him out to see what was going on. Jude had declaimed steadily ahead, and was continuing:

'*Crucifixus etiam pro nobis: sub Pontio Pilato passus, et sepultus est. Et resurrexit tertia die, secundum Scripturas.*'

'That's the Nicene,' sneered the second undergraduate. 'And we wanted the Apostles!'

'You didn't say so! And every fool knows, except you, that the Nicene is the most historic creed!'

'Let un go on, let un go on!' said the auctioneer.

But Jude's mind seemed to grow confused soon, and he could not get on. He put his hand to his forehead, and his face assumed an expression of pain.

'Give him another glass – then he'll fetch up and get through it,' said Tinker Taylor.

Somebody threw down threepence, the glass was handed, Jude stretched out his arm for it without looking, and having swallowed the liquor, went on in a moment in a revived voice, raising it as he neared the end with the manner of a priest leading a congregation:

'*Et in Spiritum Sanctum, Dominum et vivificantem, qui ex Patre Filioque procedit. Qui cum Patre et Filio simul adoratur et conglorificatur, qui locutus est per prophetas.*'

'*Et unam Catholicam et Apostolicam Ecclesiam. Confiteor unum baptisma in remissionem peccatorum. Et expecto Resurrectionem mortuorum. Et vitam venturi saeculi. Amen.*'

'Well done!' said several, enjoying the last word, as being the first and only one they had recognized.

Then Jude seemed to shake the fumes from his brain, as he stared round upon them.

'You pack of fools!' he cried. 'Which one of you knows whether I have said it or no? It might have been the Ratcatcher's Daughter in double Dutch for all that your besotted heads can tell! See what I have brought myself to – the crew I have come among!'

The landlord, who had already had his license endorsed for harbouring queer characters, feared a riot, and came outside the counter; but Jude, in his sudden flash of reason, had turned in disgust and left the scene, the door slamming with a dull thud behind him.

(Part II, Chapter 7)

Each of the six parts of *Jude the Obscure* carries a title that includes one of the place-names, fictitious but readily identifiable with actual places, belonging to the region that Hardy had come to refer to as 'Wessex'. These indications of a shifting locale, unparalleled anywhere in Hardy's earlier novels, underline the rootless nature of Jude's life: he has never had a home, and never finds one to the day of his death. Part II is titled 'At Christminster', and that city, based on Oxford, has been the goal of Jude's ambitions since an early stage in his story. But though he is now *at* Christminster, he is not really *of* it, at least if the name is to be taken as also designating the ancient university.

What he has discovered is that the city has two faces, 'town and gown', in some respects interdependent but also opposed to each other and, so far as the residents are concerned, mutually exclusive. There are the colleges, founded centuries earlier as centres of learning for poor men but now to a large extent little more than finishing schools for young men from the privileged classes. And there is the rest of the city, including a substantial working-class population, which exists partly to provide services for the university but inhabits an entirely different social and economic world as well as different districts of the city.

Jude has hoped to gain admission to the university but finds himself instead forced to take employment as a manual worker. Though he passes his days in close physical proximity to the colleges, he has no hopes of entering their gates, despite being better qualified to do so than most of the undergraduates, and this knowledge fills him with bitterness and frustration. In the scene depicted in the above passage, he gives vent to these feelings in a pub which also has among its customers some undergraduates – a pub being one of the very few places where members of the different classes could meet on a basis that was, temporarily, more or less equal. (One of the ironies of the situation is that these particular undergraduates are not serious students but playboys whose conversation concerns dogs kept for sporting purposes.)

Jude has already had too much to drink, and his tendency to turn to alcohol in moments of despair or depression is a recurring motif in the novel. The Old Testament story of Samson and Delilah is more than once invoked by Hardy in this connection: Samson was the strong man who was deprived of his powers by a woman while under the influence of drink, and the parallel with Jude and Arabella is obvious. Towards the end of the novel she will again get him drunk in order to reassert her power over him. In the scene now under discussion, the alcohol has the effect of loosening his tongue, and he returns to his obsession (what Hardy calls his 'mechanical craze') with regard to the injustice of his own exclusion from the university.

After the opening paragraph, providing the general context of the situation, most of the passage consists of dialogue, and part of its effectiveness is derived from the way in which Hardy plays off the various 'voices' against one another. Jude's Standard English, and later his recitations in Latin, are in contrast to the more homely and local speech of such characters as Tinker Taylor, Uncle Joe and the auctioneer, who use such non-standard expressions and forms as 'fetch up' for 'recover', 'Canst' for 'Can you', and 'un' for 'him'. These differentiations of speech help to create the sense of a remarkable social mix in the pub in question. Its inhabitants range from the undergraduates (who are probably there in defiance of college rules, since the pub has a bad reputation) to respectable working men like the 'surplice-maker' (dependent on the colleges for his livelihood) and Jude himself. Lower down the scale of respectability is the amusingly named 'Bower o' Bliss' (obviously well-known to at least one of the undergraduates) and the other 'ladies', who are evidently part-time prostitutes. What these different members of Jude's audience have in common is that none can really appreciate the quality of his learning, and Jude is bitterly aware of this, as his contemptuous reference to the creeds indicates. (For a comment on the Nicene creed, see p. 44 above.)

The most striking contrast within the dialogue is between the commonplace and realistic comments of the listeners and Jude's formal delivery of the majestic and sonorous Latin sentences (at one point he speaks 'with the manner of a priest leading a congregation'). The usual setting for such a performance is, of course, a church, and the usual speaker a clergyman in all the dignity of his clerical office and attire. There is thus a grim incongruity in the recitation of the creed by Jude (who wanted to be, but never will be, a clergyman) in the banal setting of a low-class pub. This is in fact the nearest Jude will ever get to attaining his ambition of entering the church.

A sudden awareness ('sudden flash of reason') of how he has betrayed his ideals by consenting to put on such a performance in such a setting, and before such a company, fills him with disgust, and self-disgust, and the scene ends dramatically with the slamming of the door as he leaves in haste. This gesture represents his rejection of the working-class pub and the way of life it represents. And yet Jude can claim admission to no superior way of life, certainly not to that of the university. In a city that includes two distinct communities, he belongs to neither.

The Mayor of Casterbridge: Communal Punishment

This novel traces the rise and fall of the protagonist, Michael Henchard, who is, at different stages of his life, both outsider and insider. As we saw earlier, the novel opens with Henchard and his family

tramping along a road, having left one home and not yet having
arrived at another. Impulsively ridding himself of his family, he
settles in Casterbridge and over a period of some twenty years not
only establishes himself as resident and successful business man in
that relatively small and closely-knit community, but becomes its
chief citizen or mayor. But his fortunes, both commercial and personal, suffer a series of setbacks, and he ends as he began, as a
wanderer, this time rejected by the community that had formerly
respected and honoured him.

The following passage describes one of the events that bring about
this radical change in Henchard's situation. The past catches up with
him after some of the townsfolk come to hear of his former irregular
liaison with the exotically named Lucetta Le Sueur (she later adopts
the name Templeman), who is now respectably married to his business rival Farfrae. Some of the rougher elements among the population decide to stage a 'skimmington ride', a traditional and noisy
demonstration of communal disapproval of immorality in which
figures resembling the offenders are paraded through the town
(more precise details of this folk-custom are given in the passage
below). The situation is thus one in which one section of the community turns against another: specifically, the slum-dwellers against
their social superiors. The result is to cause devastation in the lives of
all the principal characters.

The reverie in which these and other subjects mingled was disturbed
by a hubbub in the distance, that increased moment by moment. It
did not greatly surprise [Lucetta], the afternoon having been given
up to recreation by a majority of the populace since the passage of
the Royal equipages. But her attention was at once riveted to the
matter by the voice of a maid-servant next door, who spoke from an
upper window across the street to some other maid even more
elevated than she.

'Which way be they going now?' inquired the first with interest.

'I can't be sure for a moment,' said the second, 'because of the
malter's chimbley [chimney]. O yes – I can see 'em. Well, I declare, I
declare!'

'What, what?' from the first, more enthusiastically.

'They are coming up Corn Street after all! They sit back to back!'

'What – two of 'em – are there two figures?'

'Yes. Two images on a donkey, back to back, their elbows tied to one another's! She's facing the head, and he's facing the tail.'

'Is it meant for anybody in particular?'

'Well – it mid be. The man has got on a blue coat and kerseymere leggings; he has black whiskers, and a reddish face. 'Tis a stuffed figure, with a false face.'

The din was increasing now – then it lessened a little.

'There – I shan't see, after all!' cried the disappointed first maid.

'They have gone into a back street – that's all,' said the one who occupied the enviable position in the attic. 'There – now I have got 'em all endways nicely!'

'What's the woman like? Just say, and I can tell in a moment if 'tis meant for one I've in mind.'

'My – why – 'tis dressed just as *she* was dressed when she sat in the front seat at the time the play-actors came to the Town Hall!'

Lucetta started to her feet, and almost at the instant the door of the room was quickly and softly opened. Elizabeth-Jane advanced into the firelight.

'I have come to see you,' she said breathlessly. 'I did not stop to knock – forgive me! I see you have not shut your shutters, and the window is open.'

Without waiting for Lucetta's reply she crossed quickly to the window and pulled out one of the shutters. Lucetta glided to her side. 'Let it be – hush!' she said peremptorily, in a dry voice, while she seized Elizabeth-Jane by the hand, and held up her finger. Their intercourse had been so low and hurried that not a word had been lost of the conversation without, which had thus proceeded: –

'Her neck is uncovered, and her hair in bands, and her back-comb in place; she's got on a puce silk, and white stockings, and coloured shoes.'

Again Elizabeth-Jane attempted to close the window, but Lucetta held her by main force.

''Tis me!' she said, with a face pale as death. 'A procession – a scandal – an effigy of me, and him!'

The look of Elizabeth betrayed that the latter knew it already.

'Let us shut it out,' coaxed Elizabeth-Jane, noting that the rigid wildness of Lucetta's features was growing yet more rigid and wild with the nearing of the noise and laughter. 'Let us shut it out!'

'It is no use!' she shrieked. 'He will see it, won't he? Donald will see it! He is just coming home – and it will break his heart – he will never love me any more – and O, it will kill me – kill me!'

Elizabeth-Jane was frantic now. 'O, can't something be done to stop it?' she cried. 'Is there nobody to do it – not one?'

She relinquished Lucetta's hands, and ran to the door. Lucetta herself, saying recklessly 'I will see it!' turned to the window, threw up the sash, and went out upon the balcony. Elizabeth immediately followed, and put her arm round her to pull her in. Lucetta's eyes were straight upon the spectacle of the uncanny revel, now advancing rapidly. The numerous lights round the two effigies threw them up into lurid distinctness; it was impossible to mistake the pair for other than the intended victims.

'Come in, come in,' implored Elizabeth; 'and let me shut the window!'

'She's me – she's me – even to the parasol – my green parasol!' cried Lucetta with a wild laught as she stepped in. She stood motionless for one second – then fell heavily to the floor.

Almost at the instant of her fall the rude music of the skimmington ceased.

(Chapter 39)

Hardy's primary task in this passage is to convey the effect of the skimmington ride upon Lucetta. She has been sitting quietly and at peace, but the discovery that the community knows her guilty secret and that she is being exposed to public ridicule and humiliation produces a profound shock that has serious and ultimately fatal results. Hardy could simply have made Lucetta look out of the window and view the procession, but his narrative is conducted more indirectly and in a way that effectively uses ironic contrast. The procession is seen by the two servants, for whom it is no more than an object of curiosity and a subject of gossip; and it is through their exchanged remarks that the reader forms a clear mental picture of the centre-piece of the procession. (The vast majority of Hardy's readers would have had no better idea than their modern counterparts of the precise nature of this ancient custom.) Lucetta, however, overhears their conversation (overhearing, like spying or observing from a place of concealment, being a favourite Hardyan narrative strategy), and there is a strong contrast between the relaxed enjoyment of the servants and the dramatic horror of their employer's reaction.

Hardy then adds a further element of drama by having Elizabeth-Jane enter the room at the very moment Lucetta realizes that she herself is represented by one of the figures. Elizabeth-Jane does not speak, but her attempt to shut out the scene is eloquent: it is obvious that she knows what is going on and wishes to shield her friend from it. Lucetta, too, resorts to body language, seizing the other's hand and holding up a finger to enjoin silence. Hardy is a master of dialogue, and it is used to good effect in the earlier part of this passage; but there are times when speech is avoided or minimalized – moments when actions speak louder than words.

In the second half of the passage there is a strong sense of the narrative working towards a climax. Actually it is a double climax, involving both what is happening inside the room and what is taking place in the streets outside. Inside, the behaviour of the two women becomes more and more frenzied, as Lucetta hysterically insists on knowing the worst while Elizabeth-Jane tries in vain to discourage her. Hardy conveys this frenzy and hysteria through a series of emphatic words and phrases: 'shrieked', 'recklessly', 'by main force', 'pale as death', 'with a wild laugh', are all applied to Lucetta, while Elizabeth-Jane, at first coaxing the other, soon becomes 'frantic' herself.

Simultaneously, outside the enclosed space of the room, the raucous din of the procession – a source of malicious fun to its perpetrators – grows ever noisier: the 'noise and laughter', at first 'nearing', is soon 'advancing rapidly'. As so often, Hardy resorts to a painterly technique in showing the figures thrown into 'lurid distinctness' by illumination: the effect of light and shadow is comparable to the *chiaroscuro* of an artist such as Rembrandt, with whose work Hardy would have been very familiar both from his frequenting of the London galleries and from his travels in Holland.

The scene concludes with a double climax as Lucetta loses consciousness and the noise abruptly ceases. Both events stimulate the reader's curiosity as we wonder what will now happen to Lucetta (and also whether, as she feared, her husband has learned what is going on) and why the ride has come so suddenly to an end.

This is a scene of high drama and a turning-point in the story, and its main thrust is the demonstration of the way in which the past so often catches up with us (precisely as it does for Henchard himself when the furmity-woman discloses the wife-selling of long ago). It is, however, interesting to note how the psychological realism is reinforced by the realistic depiction of the external world, especially in this case of articles of clothing and aspects of physical appearance. First the maid enumerates the features that enable onlookers to identify the male effigy as intended to represent Henchard; later Lucetta gives an impassioned catalogue of the aspects of the female effigy that clearly resemble her own appearance; and finally, in a touching and telling detail, she refers to the 'green parasol', as if this were somehow the last straw and the ultimate indignity. Even Hardy's most dramatic scenes tend to have this underpinning of domestic realism: intense emotions and crises of experience are placed in the context of the familiar and the humdrum.

Conclusions

In the earliest of the four novels, *Far from the Madding Crowd*, the idea of community is still a living reality: the great barn, associated with communal tasks prescribed by the natural revolution of the seasons, has effectively outlived both the castle and the church, representing respectively military power and religious faith. (The message is similar to that in one of Hardy's best-known poems, 'In Time of "The Breaking of Nations"', where he suggests that rural activities 'go onward the same / Though Dynasties pass'.) In a hierarchical and enclosed society there is no sense of class struggle or of the wish to escape, though some movement within the social order is possible: inheritance enables Bathsheba to acquire wealth and influence, and Gabriel's status fluctuates as he descends from self-employment to being a hireling.

In the passage from *Tess*, on the other hand, tradition is represented by the club-walking ceremony, which survives precariously, and only in one community. The implication is that an entire culture is in the process of disintegration, and Tess's subsequent experiences, which take her farther and farther from Marlott, reinforce this idea.

Tradition survives, too, in Casterbridge in the form of the skimming-ton ride, but it is made clear that this somewhat primitive ritual is perpetuated only by those who, as slum-dwellers or petty criminals, are marginalized by the rest of society. It may be significant that the victims of the ritual, Henchard and Lucetta, have not been born into the community but both come from elsewhere.

By the time we reach *Jude*, the process of disintegration is virtually complete, and Jude, who has abandoned the countryside for the town, belongs to no community, either rural or urban. The scene in which he recites the Creed is set not in a home but a pub, and it is very different from the village inns (such as Warren's Malthouse in *Far from the Madding Crowd*) in which a group intimately known to each other regularly gather. There is no real contact or community between the various individuals in the Christminster pub – the undergraduates, the working men, the prostitutes and Jude himself – who simply happen to be in the same place at the same time. The working-class men and women seem to exist to serve the needs of the non-productive undergraduates who are themselves no perma-nent members of the community but are merely, so to speak, passing through on the way to lives that will be spent elsewhere. By the time he wrote *Jude*, at the end of his career as a novelist, Hardy had travelled a very long way from the portrayal of a community with a common purpose and a shared sense of belonging such as is depicted in *Far from the Madding Crowd*. His vision is now of the individual adrift and isolated: the community of which he or she was once a member, with a recognized role and enduring relationships, has ceased to exist. Jude himself, whose life has been driven by a quest for purposeful existence, is marginalized in the role of unwitting entertainer for those who have no appreciation of the values he has espoused.

Methods of Analysis

Most novels present both individual characters and social groups; Victorian fiction in particular tends to depict its characters as mem-bers of communities, and to present the complex interactions between different social, economic and occupational groups. In examining these passages we have paid special attention to the interaction (or lack of it) between individuals and the societies of which they are permanent or temporary members. Such interaction may be harmonious (as in the passage from *Far from the Madding Crowd*), antagonistic (*The Mayor of Casterbridge*), or virtually non-existent (*Jude the Obscure*). One obvious deduction from this is that, in considering characters in the novel, attention needs to be paid not only to internal qualities (moral, psychological, intellectual) but to relationships with other people within a social framework.

Suggestions for Further Work

The scene in Warren's Malthouse mentioned above (*Far from the Madding Crowd*, Chapter 8) is well worth examining from this point of view. The idea of community, and the role of individuals within the community, is particularly strong in *The Mayor of Casterbridge*: see, for example, Chapter 8, where the young stranger Donald Farfrae – later to become chief citizen of the town – becomes acquainted with the Casterbridge folk gathered at the Three Mariners inn. A more wide-ranging examination could be made of the early chapters of *Tess* with a view to ascertaining the role of the Durbeyfield family in the rural community: they are an ancient family long established in the district but driven to leave it by economic necessity. This theme is further developed in *Jude*, and here consideration could be given to the various kinds of community in which Jude first seeks and then fails to find a place: the village of Marygreen, the community of scholars in the academic world of Christminster, the brotherhood of fellow-workmen (Jude becomes a casual worker in a variety of places), and so forth.

5

Tradition and Change

Introduction

Hardy's major novels depict a rural society in the process of trans-formation as a result of the unprecedented social, economic and technological changes that took place in nineteenth-century England. Characteristically he portrays a traditional world only to demonstrate how it is being undermined and ultimately destroyed by the agents of change. These latter may be new inventions such as the steam-train and the kind of agricultural machine that made obsolete traditional methods of farming, or, more intangibly, the dispersal of the once tightly-knit village community and the collapse of the old social hierarchies. The following passages all illustrate different aspects of change, as a community that has formerly been relatively isolated and self- sufficient suffers the invasion of what, in another novel (*The Return of the Native*), Hardy calls 'the irrepressible New'.

Tess of the d'Urbervilles: the Two Worlds of Country and City

In this passage Tess and Angel have made the journey from Tal-bothays Dairy Farm to the nearest country railway station, in order to deliver the milk for conveyance to London. Briefly and indirectly, therefore, these two inhabitants of a secluded rural world come into contact with the city, far away but linked to them by the compara-tively new phenomenon of the railway, which in a few years had transformed the rhythms of English life and gone far towards destroying traditional lifestyles.

They crept along towards a point in the expanse of shade just at hand at which a feeble light was beginning to assert its presence, a spot where, by day, a fitful white streak of steam at intervals upon the dark green background denoted intermittent moments of contact between their secluded world and modern life. Modern life stretched out its steam feeler to this point three or four times a day, touched the native existences, and quickly withdrew its feeler again, as if what it touched had been uncongenial.

They reached the feeble light, which came from the smoky lamp of a little railway station; a poor enough terrestrial star, yet in one sense of more importance to Talbothays Dairy and mankind than the celestial ones to which it stood in such humiliating contrast. The cans of new milk were unladen in the rain, Tess getting a little shelter from a neighbouring holly tree.

Then there was the hissing of a train, which drew up almost silently upon the wet rails, and the milk was rapidly swung can by can into the truck. The light of the engine flashed for a second upon Tess Durbeyfield's figure, motionless under the great holly tree. No object could have looked more foreign to the gleaming cranks and wheels than this unsophisticated girl, with the round bare arms, the rainy face and hair, the suspended attitude of a friendly leopard at pause, the print gown of no date or fashion, and the cotton bonnet drooping on her brow.

She mounted again beside her lover, with a mute obedience characteristic of impassioned natures at times, and when they had wrapped themselves up over head and ears in the sail-cloth again, they plunged back into the now thick night. Tess was so receptive that the few minutes of contact with the whirl of material progress lingered in her thought.

'Londoners will drink it at their breakfast tomorrow, won't they?' she asked. 'Strange people that we have never seen.'

'Yes – I suppose they will. Though not as we send it. When its strength has been lowered, so that it may not get up into their heads.'

'Noble men and noble women, ambassadors and centurions, ladies and tradeswomen, and babies who have never seen a cow.'

'Well, yes, perhaps; particularly centurions.'

'Who don't know anything of us, and where it comes from; or think
how we two drove miles across the moor tonight in the rain that it
might reach 'em in time?'

'We did not drive entirely on account of these precious Londoners;
we drove a little on our own – on account of that anxious matter which
you will, I am sure, set at rest, dear Tess. Now, permit me to put it in
this way. You belong to me already, you know; your heart, I mean.
Does it not?'

(Chapter 30)

The context of this passage is the development of the love
between Tess and Angel when they are both working at Talbothays
Farm. This location, in the 'Valley of the Great Dairies', is a place of
great beauty and tranquillity, and the season of growth and fertility
enhances its idyllic quality. The methods of dairy-farming in use,
including milking and butter-making by hand, are traditional, as are
the costumes and lifestyles of the dairymaids, and one would hardly
guess that the Victorian age, with its manifold transformations, is in
full swing. The rapidly growing cities seem a world away, as if
removed in time as well as space.

In the scene described here, however, the lovers briefly emerge
from this timeless and 'secluded world' to make contact, however
indirectly, with 'modern life'. Both the phrases quoted occur in the
first paragraph, where Hardy begins – very characteristically – by
introducing the element of modernity not as a concept but as a
picture, the 'white streak of steam...upon the dark green background'. This is the railway, which by the middle of the century
had penetrated even such remote spots as Hardy's Dorset. Its unprecedented speed and cheapness produced a new relationship between
city and country, and in this instance the milk from the dairy is being
dispatched to London for consumption by city-dwellers who have
little or no knowledge of rural ways of life. Tess has never been to
London and has only vague ideas of the city and its inhabitants, as
becomes clear in the ensuing dialogue.

Hardy skilfully creates the atmosphere of the scene by the accu-
mulation of visual and other details. One striking aspect of the visual
presentation is the use of what in painting is called *chiaroscuro* (see

p. 104 above): the 'feeble light' in the 'expanse of shade' is soon identified as emanating from the 'smoky lamp' in the railway station. The 'hissing' of the train reminds us that this massive and noisy piece of machinery, which must have made such a deep impression on those seeing and hearing it for the first time, is an intruder in the countryside and produces a sound not to be found in nature. (Steam trains were much noisier as well as dirtier than their modern counterparts.) The 'light of the engine', which flashes upon Tess as she stands in the darkness, provides another vivid visual touch. Hardy stresses the contrast between the figure of Tess, in her gown and bonnet of traditional style, and the machine that is the symbol of change and modernity: 'No object could have looked more foreign...'.

We also find here another instance of what has already been referred to as the 'cinematic' element in Hardy's descriptive technique. The 'streak of steam' seen against 'a dark green background' is striking in several ways. In purely visual terms it offers a chromatic contrast of white against green. In much broader terms, the contrast is between worlds and epochs, the Industrial Age represented by the steam-train and the Agrarian Age that has preceded it: in other words it embodies an idea as well as an image. The bird's-eye view or aerial shot with which the description begins gives the sense of a whole stretch of landscape, but soon moves into close-up as we are shown the 'little railway station' deserted except for Tess and Angel. There is also an implied visual contrast between the commonplace 'smoky lamp' of the station and the 'celestial' lights – that is, the stars in the heavens – that are part of the larger scene. The life-spans of Tess and Angel may be small in comparison with the great movements of history, not to mention prehistory and geological time, just as their physical size is dwarfed by the scene in which they are placed. But they are at the centre of that scene, and they are given significance and dignity by their capacity for feeling and for suffering. Hardy seems to be offering the paradox that the apparently smaller can actually be the greater.

A similar technique is used in *The Mayor of Casterbridge*, where the individual destiny of Henchard is played out among scenes that constantly recall the past, and often the very distant past, even while he is caught up in a rapidly changing modern world. As we have seen, both *The Mayor of Casterbridge* and *The Return of the Native* open with aerial or long-distance 'shots' that similarly challenge us to reflect on the relative significance of the human and the non-human elements.

Hardy is thus bringing together elements of very different kinds and belonging to entirely different scales: a broad landscape and the sky above, a banal modern intrusion in the form of a railway station, and two human individuals. It might seem at first as if the larger physical context reduces the human element into insignificance, but it can be argued that exactly the opposite is the case.

The latter part of the passage offers another kind of contrast, between Tess, with her naive notions of the city (Hardy has already applied to her the epithet 'unsophisticated') and Angel, who is an educated man from a middle-class background (his father is a clergyman). Tess, though lacking in knowledge and experience, is imaginative and speculates on the gulf that divides her world from that of those who will drink the milk she has extracted from the cows. Her enumeration of different types of city-dweller draws on the vocabulary of story-books and has little appropriateness to actual life: 'Noble men and noble women, ambassadors and centurions...'. 'Centurions', of course, is a slightly ludicrous term in this context: Hardy no doubt means us to suppose that Tess has met the word somewhere in her reading, probably at the 'National School' she has attended, but is unaware that it refers to the Roman army of the ancient world, not the British army of the nineteenth century. Angel, well aware of her blunder, tactfully avoids pointing out her mistake but allows himself a gentle irony in his reply ('particularly centurions').

Tess's last speech in the extract quoted reveals her sensitivity and her consciousness that her own world is far removed from that on which she has been speculating. The passage as a whole draws attention to the isolation of the world inhabited by Tess and Angel at this stage of the story. Isolated and united by their love for each other, they are doubly isolated by their life on the dairy farm in a district remote from urban centres. For a few moments the train forms a link between them and a larger world, and to this extent it is comparable to the human invaders who play so important a role in many of Hardy's plots. (Alec d'Urberville is an obvious case in point, and Angel too must be counted as an outsider.) As the story unfolds, it becomes clear that the Talbothays idyll cannot last: just as the season of warmth and growth gives way to winter, Tess will find herself cast out into a harsher existence in which the forces of the outside world cannot be escaped. The later stages of Tess's brief life take her to urban rather than rural scenes (Sandbourne, where she lives with Alec, is based on the rapidly expanding holiday resort of Bournemouth). Ultimately, with her trial and execution, the highly organized world of a complex modern society takes control of her fate.

Jude the Obscure: Change in the Village

The following extract from the opening pages of Hardy's last novel presents the hero as a child growing up in a small village. He is an orphan and almost entirely lacks the ties, human and otherwise, that normally connect us to the past. But the village too has suffered changes that have gone far towards entirely destroying the evidences of its historic past, so that there is an important relationship between the situation of the protagonist and the broader historical and cultural frame within which he lives.

The cart creaked across the green, and disappeared round the corner by the rectory-house. The boy returned to the draw-well at the edge of the greensward, where he had left his buckets when he went to help his patron and teacher in the loading. There was a quiver in his lip now, and after opening the well-cover to begin lowering the bucket he paused and leant with his forehead and arms against the framework, his face wearing the fixity of a thoughtful child's who has felt the pricks of life somewhat before his time. The well into which he was looking was as ancient as the village itself, and from his present position appeared as a long circular perspective ending in a shining disk of quivering water at a distance of a hundred feet down. There was a lining of green moss near the top, and nearer still the hart's-tongue fern.

He said to himself, in the melodramatic tones of a whimsical boy, that the schoolmaster had drawn at that well scores of times on a morning like this, and would never draw there any more. 'I've seen him look down into it, when he was tired with his drawing, just as I do now, and when he rested a bit before carrying the buckets home! But he was too clever to bide here any longer – a small sleepy place like this!'

A tear rolled from his eye into the depths of the well. The morning was a little foggy, and the boy's breathing unfurled itself as a thicker fog upon the still and heavy air. His thoughts were interrupted by a sudden outcry:

'Bring on that water, will ye, you idle young harlican!'

It came from an old woman who had emerged from her door towards the garden gate of a green-thatched cottage not far off. The boy quickly waved a signal of assent, drew the water with what was a great effort for one of his stature, landed and emptied the big bucket into his own pair of smaller ones, and pausing a moment for breath, started with them across the patch of clammy greensward whereon the well stood – nearly in the centre of the little village, or rather hamlet of Marygreen.

It was as old-fashioned as it was small, and it rested in the lap of an undulating upland adjoining the North Wessex downs. Old as it was, however, the well-shaft was probably the only relic of the local history that remained absolutely unchanged. Many of the thatched and dor- mered dwelling-houses had been pulled down of late years, and many trees felled on the green. Above all, the original church, hump-backed, wood-turreted, and quaintly hipped, had been taken down, and either cracked up into heaps of road-metal in the lane, or utilized as pig-sty walls, garden seats, guard-stones to fences, and rockeries in the flower- beds of the neighbourhood. In place of it a tall new building of modern Gothic design, unfamiliar to English eyes, had been erected on a new piece of ground by a certain obliterator of historic records who had run down from London and back in a day. The site whereon so long had stood the ancient temple to the Christian divinities was not even recorded on the green and level grass-plot that had immemorially been the churchyard, the obliterated graves being commemorated by eighteen-penny cast-iron crosses warranted to last five years.

(Part I, Chapter 1)

Jude Fawley, the last of Hardy's heroes, is also the one whose life is most deeply influenced by the forces of change at work in Victorian England. At the beginning of the novel he is a child, an orphan living with a great-aunt in the village of Marygreen. (The fictional village is based on Great Fawley in Oxfordshire, which not only provided Jude's surname but had strong personal associations for Hardy, one of whose grandmothers was brought up there.) A clever and sensitive child, Jude knows he is not wanted by his elderly relative, to whom he is an economic and emotional burden. He senses, indeed, that he really has no place in the world. The rest of the novel traces his search for such a place – a search that is unsuccessful and ends only in despair and death.

The cart that disappears from the scene in the opening sentence of the extract is carrying away the possessions of the village school-master who has befriended Jude and has been 'his patron and teacher', but who has now moved away. The 'quiver in his lip' is silent evidence – soon to be reinforced by his spoken words – of Jude's sadness at the departure of the man who has been his only friend. When Jude looks down the circular well, it is as if it were a telescope through which he is attempting to see what the future holds for him. Hardy also stresses the extreme antiquity of the well ('as ancient as the village itself'), preparing the reader for the fuller exposition a little later of the ways in which the long-established traditions of the community are being eroded and destroyed by modern change.

If the well seems to carry a symbolic significance, however, the prevailing method of the passage, as of this novel as a whole, is one of high realism. The language is for the most part concrete, making use of such homely objects as the 'cart', the 'buckets' and the 'well-cover', and there are precise descriptions of the visual elements in the scene, including the moss and fern growing in the well and the child's breath visible in the cold morning air.

Jude's melancholy and regretful meditations are interrupted by a brusque cry, the voice of his great-aunt ordering him to get a move on with the water-supply. (She is economically characterized by her use of the dialect term 'harlican', meaning something like 'rascal' or 'good-for-nothing' and suggestive of a somewhat harsh attitude towards the child she is bringing up.) The reader's sympathies are very much with Jude, and the narrative encourages us to feel for his situation in both its emotional and its physical dimensions. His feelings, unappreciated by his great-aunt or anyone else left in the village, are all the more poignant for having no remedy; at the same time Hardy gives details of the physical location and atmosphere that enable us to feel imaginatively the coldness of the morning air, the heaviness of the buckets of water, and the 'clammy greensward' Jude walks across on his heavily-laden way to the cottage.

Jude's slow progress to the cottage marks the end of the narrative in this opening chapter. But Hardy adds a long final paragraph of narratorial commentary that contextualizes the simple events that have been described. And here the narrator's tone is strikingly different from that of the earlier part of the excerpt. Jude's unhappy state of mind has been presented with compassion but without sentimentality, and indeed with a degree of detachment: in, for instance, the sentence beginning 'There was a quiver in his lip...', his posture is described with objective precision, and there is a certain formality in the classification of Jude as 'a thoughtful child...who has felt the pricks of life somewhat before his time' ('pricks', in the sense of hardships or pains, is an archaic word with Biblical associations).

In the final paragraph, however, the tone becomes critical and ironic as the theme shifts from the unhappy child to the way in which village life is being destroyed in modern England. The opening sentence, which places Marygreen geographically, has a guide-book quality, but thereafter there are strong implications of disapproval in the account of the way in which the village has suffered from the winds of change. Both architecture and the natural environment have suffered, with cottages being demolished and trees felled. The fullest protest is directed at the 'restoration' of the ancient church, which – like thousands of others in Victorian England – has been extensively rebuilt.

As a professional architect, Hardy had himself specialized in church restoration (see p. 162 below) – had been, in the phrase of this passage, an 'obliterator of historic records' – and a certain amount of guilt may have been mixed with his indignation in his attack upon this practice. His expert knowledge of architecture is evident in his use of such technical terms as 'hipped' (with a projecting edge). But although the language has a factual exactness, some of the images evoked can also be interpreted as metaphors or symbols. The very stones of the old church, built in an age of faith, have been broken up and put to practical and secular use in the making of roads, pigsties, rockeries and so forth; and this surely suggests the secularization of life in modern England, where the church no longer enjoys the centrality it formerly had in personal and community life. Even the graveyard, potent symbol of the relationship of the living with the dead, has been 'obliterated'; the gravestones, individually carved by local craftsmen, have given place to cheap 'cast-iron crosses' that are obviously the products of a factory.

Hardy makes it clear that it is the past itself, and all that links the living with their forebears, that has been destroyed. Jude himself is a typical product of such a generation, virtually deprived of a past by the absence of family and with no sense of belonging to any place that has important personal associations for him. Thus, what looks like a digression in this final paragraph turns out to have a close connection with the plight of the central character and to contextualize personal experience in relation to the broader history of the times.

The Mayor of Casterbridge: the Mechanization of Farming

In the following passage, 'change' is presented as no mere abstraction but in the form of a piece of farm machinery that will revolutionize farming methods. Its advent is responded to in different ways by the two principal male characters of the novel, rivals in business as well as in love, and Hardy uses the horse-drill, an object of keen public curiosity in Casterbridge, as a device for bringing together a group of people whose emotional lives and ultimate fates are closely intertwined.

> The morning was exceptionally bright for the time of year. The sun fell so flat on the houses and pavement opposite Lucetta's residence that they poured their brightness into her rooms. Suddenly, after a rumbling of wheels, there were added to this steady light a fantastic series of circling irradiations upon the ceiling, and the companions turned to

the window. Immediately opposite a vehicle of strange description had come to a standstill, as if it had been placed there for exhibition.

It was the new-fashioned agricultural implement called a horse-drill, till then unknown, in its modern shape, in this part of the country, where the venerable seed-lip was still used for sowing as in the days of the Heptarchy. Its arrival created about as much sensation in the corn-market as a flying machine would create at Charing Cross. The farmers crowded round it, women drew near it, children crept under and into it. The machine was painted in bright hues of green, yellow, and red, and it resembled as a whole a compound of hornet, grasshopper, and shrimp, magnified enormously. Or it might have been likened to an upright musical instrument with the front gone. That was how it struck Lucetta. 'Why, it is a sort of agricultural piano,' she said.

'It has something to do with corn,' said Elizabeth.

'I wonder who thought of introducing it here?'

Donald Farfrae was in the minds of both as the innovator, for though not a farmer he was closely leagued with farming operations. And as if in response to their thought he came up at that moment, looked at the machine, walked round it, and handled it as if he knew something about its make. The two watchers had inwardly started at his coming, and Elizabeth left the window, went to the back of the room, and stood as if absorbed in the panelling of the wall. She hardly knew that she had done this till Lucetta, animated by the conjunction of her new attire with the sight of Farfrae, spoke out: 'Let us go and look at the instrument, whatever it is.'

Elizabeth-Jane's bonnet and shawl were pitchforked on in a moment, and they went out. Among all the agriculturists gathered round the only appropriate possessor of the new machine seemed to be Lucetta, because she alone rivalled it in colour.

They examined it curiously; observing the rows of trumpet-shaped tubes one within the other, the little scoops, like revolving salt-spoons, which tossed the seed into the upper ends of the tubes that conducted it to the ground; till somebody said, 'Good morning, Elizabeth-Jane.' She looked up, and there was her stepfather.

His greeting had been somewhat dry and thunderous, and Elizabeth-Jane, embarrassed out of her equanimity, stammered at random, 'This is the lady I live with, father – Miss Templeman.'

Henchard put his hand to his hat, which he brought down with a great wave till it met his body at the knee. Miss Templeman bowed. 'I am happy to become acquainted with you, Mr Henchard,' she said. 'This is a curious machine.'

'Yes,' Henchard replied; and he proceeded to explain it, and still more forcibly to ridicule it.

'Who brought it here?' said Lucetta.

'Oh, don't ask me, ma'am!' said Henchard. 'The thing – why 'tis impossible it should act. 'Twas brought here by one of our machinists on the recommendation of a jumped-up jackanapes of a fellow who thinks –' His eye caught Elizabeth-Jane's imploring face, and he stopped, probably thinking that the suit might be progressing.

(Chapter 24)

In the opening paragraph of this passage Hardy sets the scene by establishing a clear sense of interior and exterior space: the privacy and seclusion of a room in Lucetta's house in the centre of Caster-bridge, and the busy street outside which can be seen from Lucetta's window. He also draws attention to the power and quality of the sunlight: as so often, Hardy's prose seems to go some way towards paralleling the work of the Impressionist painters who were his approximate contemporaries. He also refers to the 'companions', Lucetta and Elizabeth-Jane, who are to play an important part in this scene, and stimulates the reader's curiosity by referring to 'a vehicle of strange description' without at first identifying it more precisely. It is soon, however, identified as a horse-drill, a horse-drawn machine for planting seed and one example among many of the ways in which agricultural methods were becoming mechanized during the period in which the main action of the novel takes place (the 1840s, the period of Hardy's childhood).

The second paragraph allows us to see the horse-drill in close-up. But before its appearance, and its impact upon the townsfolk, are described, it is placed historically. Though not actually a new invention, it is 'till then unknown, in its modern shape, in this part of the country': up to this date the seed has been sown by hand, using a 'seed-lip' or basket carried by the sower, who would dip his hand into it and cast the seed upon the earth. Hardy might have mentioned that this was a method that went back at least to Biblical times: one of the best known of the parables of Jesus concerns the sower who 'went forth to sow'. He prefers, however, to stress the continuity of farming methods in this particular region by pointing out that the same method was used 'in the days of the Heptarchy' – that is, of the seven kingdoms, of which Wessex was one, that constituted what later became England.

It is interesting to find Hardy using, in the same sentence, words as different as 'seed-lip' and 'Heptarchy'. Both are uncommon, but they come from entirely different registers or sub-groups of vocabulary. The former refers to a simple object serving a practical purpose and would have been part of the everyday discourse of farm-workers; the other is a term used by medieval historians, belongs primarily to the written rather than the spoken language, and would be familiar to only a small, highly-educated elite. In miniature, this example illustrates the remarkable range of Hardy's vocabulary in his prose and verse.

In the streets of Casterbridge, the horse-drill creates an impression as an exotic and unfamiliar object, and Hardy brings out this reaction by stressing its garish colours, by comparing it to a living creature 'magnified enormously', and by the bizarre image of a piano with the front removed and the works exposed. The piano was at this time associated with genteel middle-class households, and appropriately enough it is the well-to-do Lucetta who describes it as 'a sort of agricultural piano'. For her, it is a mere curiosity, welcome to relieve boredom, and she fails to grasp the important fact that it has a practical use and is likely to revolutionize farming methods if it is introduced in the district.

We, and she, soon learn that it is associated with Donald Farfrae, the young man from Scotland whose knowledge of modern agricultural and business methods is setting him in rivalry with Michael Henchard. When Farfrae is spotted by the two women, Hardy gives the reader a strong sense of physical space, placing the three characters in significant relationship to each other: Farfrae is outside, and so far unaware of the women who are so conscious of his presence; Lucetta, at the window, is anxious to be seen and admired in her fashionable new dress; Elizabeth-Jane, embarrassed and unwilling to betray her feelings, withdraws to the back of the room.

It is, naturally enough, Lucetta who is responsible for the two women going out into the street: so far as she is concerned, the attraction, of course, is not the horse-drill (though she does make a superficial inspection of it) but Farfrae, and in this fact there is an implicit criticism of her life and values. She is one of the idle rich and, unlike most of the inhabitants of Casterbridge, leads a life of unproductive leisure. She is ignorant of, and indifferent to, the life and work of the town and the surrounding countryside: what she really cares more for are the latest fashions in clothes and the romantic possibilities represented by the young Scot. In Hardy's novels, those not engaged in productive labour are usually morally suspect (compare Alec d'Urberville in *Tess*), and it is not surprising that in due course Lucetta's irresponsible life catches up with her and she comes to a bad end.

The arrival of Henchard introduces a complicating element: not only is there a strained relationship between him and Elizabeth-Jane, who has left him in order to live with Lucetta, but he is the former lover of Lucetta (now passing under the assumed name of Miss Templeman), though this is not generally known. It is, therefore, a dramatic and ironic moment when Elizabeth-Jane introduces him to her friend. Hardy makes the moment visually vivid by describing the body language of the participants as well as reporting their speech: Henchard's gesture in taking off his hat suggests something of his bold and assertive nature, while Lucetta more discreetly limits herself to a formal bow.

Lucetta's diverting of the conversation to the 'curious machine' is probably a ploy to keep off more personal and potentially dangerous topics. Henchard's dismissive ridicule of the new machine reveals an important aspect of his character, his stubborn traditionalism and refusal to adapt himself to changing times. His insistence that "'tis impossible it should act', for instance, is based on prejudice rather than knowledge. It is this characteristic that is to be one of the main ingredients in his subsequent downfall. Though he does not mention Farfrae directly, he clearly has the young man in mind in his reference to 'a jumped-up jackanapes of a fellow'.

It is only the glimpse of his step-daughter's 'imploring face' that prevents Henchard from continuing his attack on Farfrae, whom he believes to be romantically interested in her. The encounter as a whole makes clear the complex network of emotional tensions existing between the four characters. It is very striking, however, that much of the communication that takes place is at a non-verbal level: in many of Hardy's most dramatic scenes, such elements as gesture and posture, and the 'reading' of a facial expression, can be as eloquent as, even more eloquent than, the words actually spoken.

Far from the Madding Crowd: the Woman Farmer

This relatively early novel is often thought of as commemorating and celebrating traditional modes of existence rather than exploring the forces that were radically transforming the England Hardy knew and wrote about. In one major respect, however, it confronts an unfamiliar phenomenon that is a portent of social change. The central figure is a woman who is also a working farmer and an employer of largely male labour. It is true that Bathsheba Everdene can hardly be classified as a 'new woman' of the self-conscious and politically aware kind that became familiar a couple of decades later and is most vividly presented in the figure of Sue Bridehead in *Jude the Obscure*. But her chosen role disturbs the status quo, as we see in this early scene in which she challengingly takes her place in the hitherto all-male commercial world of the cornmarket.

> The first public evidence of Bathsheba's decision to be a farmer in her own person and by proxy no more was her appearance the following market-day in the cornmarket at Casterbridge.
> The low though extensive hall, supported by beams and pillars, and latterly dignified by the name of Corn Exchange, was thronged with hot men who talked among each other in twos and threes, the speaker of the minute looking sideways into his auditor's face and concentrating his argument by a contraction of one eyelid during delivery. The greater number carried in their hands ground-ash saplings, using them partly as walking-sticks and partly for poking up pigs, sheep, neighbours with their backs turned, and restful things in general, which

seemed to require such treatment in the course of their peregrinations. During conversations each subjected his sapling to great varieties of usage – bending it round his back, forming an arch of it between his two hands, overweighting it on the ground till it reached nearly a semicircle; or perhaps it was hastily tucked under the arm whilst the sample-bag was pulled forth and a handful of corn poured into the palm, which, after criticism, was flung upon the floor, an issue of events perfectly well known to half-a-dozen acute town-bred fowls which had as usual crept into the building unobserved, and waited the fulfilment of their anticipations with a high-stretched neck and oblique eye.

Among these heavy yeomen a feminine figure glided, the single one of her sex that the room contained. She was prettily and even daintily dressed. She moved between them as a chaise between carts, was heard after them as a romance after sermons, was felt among them like a breeze among furnaces. It had required a little determination – far more than she had at first imagined – to take up a position here, for at her first entry the lumbering dialogues had ceased, nearly every face had been turned towards her, and those that were already turned rigidly fixed there.

Two or three only of the farmers were personally known to Bathsheba, and to these she had made her way. But if she was to be the practical woman she had intended to show herself, business must be carried on, introductions or none, and she ultimately acquired confidence enough to speak and reply boldly to men merely known to her by hearsay. Bathsheba too had her sample-bags, and by degrees adopted the professional pour into the hand – holding up the grains in her narrow palm for inspection, in perfect Casterbridge manner.

Something in the exact arch of her upper unbroken row of teeth and in the keenly pointed corners of her red mouth when, with parted lips, she somewhat defiantly turned up her face to argue a point with a tall man, suggested that there was potentiality enough in that lithe slip of humanity for alarming exploits of sex, and daring enough to carry them out. But her eyes had a softness – invariably a softness – which had they not been dark, would have seemed mistiness; as they were, it lowered an expression that might have been piercing to simple clearness.

Strange to say of a woman in full bloom and vigour, she always allowed her interlocutors to finish their statements before rejoining with hers. In arguing on prices, she held to her own firmly, as was natural in a dealer, and reduced theirs persistently, as was inevitable in a woman. But there was an elasticity in her firmness which removed it from obstinacy, as there was a *naïveté* in her cheapening which saved it from meanness.

Those of the farmers with whom she had no dealings (by far the greater part) were continually asking each other, 'Who is she?' The reply would be –

'Farmer Everdene's niece; took on Weatherbury Upper Farm; turned away the baily [bailiff], and swears she'll do everything herself.'

The other man would then shake his head.

'Yes, 'tis a pity she's so headstrong,' the first would say. 'But we ought to be proud of her here – she lightens up the old place. 'Tis such a shapely maid, however, that she'll soon get picked up.'

It would be ungallant to suggest that the novelty of her engagement in such an occupation had almost as much to do with the magnetism as had the beauty of her face and movements. However, the interest was general, and this Saturday's *début* in the forum, whatever it may have been to Bathsheba as the buying and selling farmer, was unquestionably a triumph to her as the maiden. Indeed, the sensation was so pronounced that her instinct on two or three occasions was merely to walk as a queen among these gods of the fallow, like a little sister of a little Jove, and to neglect closing prices altogether.

The numerous evidences of her power to attract were only thrown into greater relief by a marked exception. Women seem to have eyes in their ribbons for such matters as these. Bathsheba, without looking within a right angle of him, was conscious of a black sheep among the flock.

It perplexed her first. If there had been a respectable minority on either side, the case would have been most natural. If nobody had regarded her, she would have taken the matter indifferently – such cases had occurred. If everybody, this man included, she would have taken it as a matter of course – people had done so before. But the smallness of the exception made the mystery.

She soon knew thus much of the recusant's appearance. He was a gentlemanly man, with full and distinctly outlined Roman features, the prominences of which glowed in the sun with a bronze-like richness of tone. He was erect in attitude and quiet in demeanour. One characteristic pre-eminently marked him – dignity.

(Chapter 12)

In the long second paragraph of this extract, Hardy evokes the traditional all-male society of the cornmarket. For generations this assembly, in which farmers from a wide area come together to buy and sell grain, has been part of the regular pattern of commercial life in the market town and administrative centre of Casterbridge. But on this occasion there is a new and entirely unprecedented element, introduced at the beginning of the third paragraph. The emphasis falls on Bathsheba's physical difference from the heavily-built men: she 'glided' across the room, and the verb has distinct feminine connotations of lightness and delicacy of movement. She is also attractively dressed, so that her presence among the burly farmers is startling and cannot be ignored.

In a sense this emphasis on Bathsheba's femininity, to some extent of her own devising ('daintily dressed'), undermines and partially invalidates her primary intention, which is to be taken seriously and on a basis of equality as a farmer and business woman. And this conflict is also part of the narrator's stance. While he has respect for what Bathsheba is doing and obviously expects the reader to be impressed, he also makes somewhat condescending generalizations about women: the patronizing facetiousness of such a phrase as 'as was inevitable in a woman' later in the passage implies a refusal to take the heroine quite seriously in her attempt to compete on equal terms in what has traditionally been a man's world.

There is, however, a recognition that beneath the conventional feminine surface Bathsheba is a young woman of rare qualities. Her facial expression as she negotiates with the farmers suggests 'potentiality enough in that lithe slip of humanity for alarming exploits of sex'. The adjective 'alarming' in this context is unexpectedly forceful, especially in contrast to the phrase 'lithe slip' that precedes it. ('Sex' here is probably used not so much in the usual modern sense of physical sexuality as to denote specifically female powers.) The hint prepares us for some of the actions and decisions that Bathsheba is to take later in the story and which generate some of the most dramatic elements in the plot.

Hardy's prose in this passage is largely discursive and analytical: in, for instance, the paragraph beginning 'Strange to say...', the language is largely abstract and Bathsheba's nature and behaviour are described in general terms ('elasticity', 'firmness', '*naïveté*', etc.) rather than being presented through action or speech. The exception is the brief conversation between the farmers as they identify and discuss Bathsheba. Notable here is their conservative view of a woman's role: she is criticized as 'headstrong' because she is not content to accept the kind of role normally assigned to a woman: she is judged in terms of appearance rather than ability ('a shapely maid'), and it is assumed that marriage (bluntly referred to in the phrase 'picked up') is her natural destiny and will soon put a stop to her nonsense.

Again, the narrator seems to go some way towards colluding in this traditionally male attitude when he makes a distinction between the kinds of impression she has made as a 'farmer' and a 'maiden'. In discussing this passage there need be little hesitation in referring to the narrator as 'he', since the views expressed or implied are essentially masculine. Masculinity takes another form at the end of the extract with the introduction of Farmer Boldwood, a 'gentlemanly' figure who is to play an important role in the story and whose 'dignity' is to be destroyed by Bathsheba's irresponsibility.

The scene is, therefore, constructed upon contrasts, visible and invisible. In the masculine crowd Bathsheba makes an immediate impression as an incongruous figure. But her presence there, and her evident determination to conduct business herself rather than doing it through a male intermediary, imply qualities of mind and character that are to be developed subsequently both through analysis and through more dramatic modes of presentation.

As in other passages discussed, the narrator is implicitly defined as one who is well-informed about the way of life he is describing. He not only understands the significance and the procedures of the regular gatherings in the Corn Exchange but knows in intimate detail how people of this kind behave. And as usual these details are presented with sharp visual precision. He not only knows that the farmers are in the habit of carrying a ground-ash sapling but describes precisely how they hold and use it in a variety of ways. There is a similar precision in the description of the way in which the corn is poured for inspection from the sample-bags. Hardy resisted being typecast as a chronicler of rural scenes, but one can see why early readers and critics regarded this skilful evocation of a culture unfamiliar to most of them as one of his outstanding strengths as a writer.

Conclusions

In all these passages, Hardy uses contrast to stress the difference between two ways of life, one traditional but threatened, the other new and likely to destroy the older ways.

In *Far from the Madding Crowd*, the earliest of the novels discussed, the male-dominated world of Casterbridge trading in corn is challenged by an inexperienced but courageous girl, Bathsheba: the time has come, it seems, for women to play a role in the world of business as well as in the domestic sphere. In *The Mayor of Casterbridge* a piece of new agricultural machinery promises to transform methods of farming that have prevailed for centuries; its arrival also polarizes the responses of the two principal male characters, since Farfrae is prepared to welcome the new while Henchard clings stubbornly to the old. In *Tess* the lovers emerge briefly from a pastoral world to encounter the railway that links them to the busy centres of urban life. In *Jude*, the last of Hardy's novels, the village has changed radically at the hands of modernizers and hardly a trace of the old world remains except in the memory of those who, like the narrator, view change with regret, or at least with very mixed feelings.

As well as portraying the changes that are taking place, Hardy places on record the world that is vanishing or that has already vanished but survives in his memory. It is worth noting in this connection that his novels are often set at a somewhat earlier date than that of composition and publication: the main action of *The Mayor of Casterbridge*, for instance, antedates publication by about forty years, and the Casterbridge world is that remembered from Hardy's boyhood.

Methods of Analysis

As in earlier chapters, the above analyses have paid attention to the role of the narrator and his relationship to the world created by his narrative. In describing traditional ways of life and work (for instance, the transactions in the Casterbridge cornmarket) he speaks with authority, but he can also vividly depict aspects of the new, such as the horse-drill and the rebuilding of medieval churches. Although intimately familiar with the life and work of Wessex, he can also stand back and view it in the broader context available to an outsider. This is reflected in Hardy's style: his vocabulary, for instance, draws on both the specialized vocabulary of rural pursuits and a more learned or intellectual vocabulary of the kind that might be used in the London newspapers and journals.

Again, it has also proved useful to examine Hardy's pictorialism, including his techniques of placing characters in a scene (as a painter might place figures on a canvas), and his use of unusual lighting-effects. But description is of course only one of the elements in the discourse of a novel, as narratorial commentary is another, and Hardy also makes important use of dialogue to heighten moments of dramatic significance. When Tess and Angel talk about the Londoners whom they are supplying with milk, or when the farmers in the cornmarket discuss Bathsheba, or Henchard is introduced to Lucetta, attention needs to be paid to the full dramatic context – not only the words spoken but descriptions of body language and tone of voice. Sometimes most important of all are the unspoken meanings that lie beneath the surface of a banal exchange (such as the reader's knowledge that Henchard is no stranger to Lucetta but has had a sexual relationship with her).

Suggestions for Further Work

The opening paragraphs of Chapter 47 of *Tess of the d'Urbervilles* provide an example that is both striking in itself and forms an interesting comparison with the passage from *The Mayor of Casterbridge* discussed above. At this stage in her story, Tess is employed by a farmer at Flintcomb-Ash and is set to work on a steam-driven threshing-machine. The garish machine and its 'sooty and grimy' operator, who is 'in the agricultural world, but not of it', are vividly described. Consider the similarities and differences between these two presentations of newly introduced agricultural machinery.

More generally, you may like to develop the references to the railway above by finding scenes (they are quite numerous) in *Jude the Obscure* in which railways, railway journeys and associated places (for example, station platforms and station hotels) play a significant part. In the same novel, the reference to architectural history in the final paragraph of the opening chapter may be used as the starting-point for a consideration of the way in which architecture and contrasting architectural styles are used throughout *Jude*. (Look, for example, at the opening of Part III, Chapter 2, where Jude and Sue discuss the rival merits of Gothic and Classical styles; and bear in mind that the hero of this novel is a stonemason whose work involves making new buildings and restoring old ones.)

The strength of traditional ways of living, working and feeling, even when they are under threat, is a major theme in *Far from the Madding Crowd*. Consider the many different ways in which tradition is defined and exemplified in this novel. Some obvious examples are: homes and buildings; occupations and working methods; dress and ways of speech; attitudes to authority.

6

Men and Women

Introduction

All Hardy's novels are love stories, but from an early stage in his career he depicts love relationships as problematic and liable to be attended with pain, stress, and even madness and tragedy. In his second published novel, *Under the Greenwood Tree* (1872), for instance, the heroine, Fancy Day, is a young teacher who finds herself obliged to choose between three men who all seek her hand in marriage – a simple countryman, a rich farmer, and a socially superior clergyman – and the happy ending is reached only after she has confronted the opposition between the impulses of her heart and the lures of social and economic ambition. In this chapter we shall examine a number of scenes in which the relationships between men and women, inside and outside marriage, are explored.

Love and marriage have always been major themes – perhaps even *the* major themes – in the English novel. One has only to think of the tradition of writers from Jane Austen to D. H. Lawrence and beyond who have been centrally concerned with the stage in the lives of men and women when they are seeking a partner. But there were internal and external reasons why the subject appealed so strongly to Hardy in the last decades of the nineteenth century. His relationship with his wife Emma had started as a love match, but the tensions within their marriage later became acute. In the public sphere, the social and legal status of married women was widely debated and subjected to change by legislation. More broadly, agitation for (and counter-reactions to) the social and political emancipation of women became increasingly intense.

Far from the Madding Crowd: a Symbolic Seduction

The pattern established in *Under the Greenwood Tree* is repeated, but explored more thoroughly, in *Far from the Madding Crowd*, where another independent young woman, Bathsheba Everdene, is also loved by three men: Gabriel Oak, a worthy but undemonstrative shepherd; Sergeant Frank Troy, a dashing and unprincipled soldier; and William Boldwood, another prosperous farmer. As his strongly symbolic name suggests, Gabriel Oak is a fine man, with inner strength and utterly reliable, but he is quiet and modest, and can be socially inept; and though it is he who in the end wins Bathsheba, this is only accomplished after heartache and tragedy. Troy is, as a personality, Gabriel's opposite: confident, outgoing and sexually predatory, he has seduced a local girl, Fanny Robin, and now has designs upon Bathsheba.

For Hardy, however, at an early stage of his career and anxious to secure a good reputation with editors, publishers and readers, presenting Troy as the potential seducer of the heroine is a project fraught with risk. *Far from the Madding Crowd* was his first big opportunity to publish a novel in a leading London magazine, and he must have known that what he produced could make or break him. His brilliant solution to this specific problem was to write a scene that, a generation before the early writings of Freud, makes powerful use of sexual symbolism.

In the passage that follows, Troy and Bathsheba meet while out walking, and he treats her to a daring and fascinating exhibition of his skill with the sword. He is a colourful figure (soldiers wore scarlet, not khaki, at that time), and swordsmanship would have been part of his training and a matter of intense professional pride. Here, however, it is put to a different use, as a technique for seduction:

'I heard you rustling through the fern before I saw you,' he said, coming up and giving her his hand to help her down the slope.

The pit was a saucer-shaped concave, naturally formed, with a top diameter of about thirty feet, and shallow enough to allow the sunshine to reach their heads. Standing in the centre, the sky overhead was met by a circular horizon of fern: this grew nearly to the bottom of the slope and then abruptly ceased. The middle within the belt of verdure was floored with a thick flossy carpet of moss and grass intermingled, so yielding that the foot was half-buried within it.

'Now,' said Troy, producing the sword, which, as he raised it into the sunlight, gleamed a sort of greeting, like a living thing; 'first, we have four right and four left cuts; four right and four left thrusts. Infantry cuts and guards are more interesting than ours, to my mind; but they are not so swashing. They have seven cuts and three thrusts. So much as a preliminary. Well, next, our cut one is as if you were sowing your corn – so.' Bathsheba saw a sort of rainbow, upside down in the air, and Troy's arm was still again. 'Cut two, as if you were hedging – so. Three, as if you were reaping – so. Four, as if you were threshing – in that way. Then the same on the left. The thrusts are these: one, two, three, four, right; one, two, three, four, left.' He repeated them. 'Have 'em again?' he said. 'One, two –'

She hurriedly interrupted: 'I'd rather not; though I don't mind your twos and fours; but your ones and threes are terrible!'

'Very well. I'll let you off the ones and threes. Next, cuts, points, and guards altogether.' Troy duly exhibited them. 'Then there's pursuing practice, in this way.' He gave the movements as before. 'There, those are the stereotyped forms. The infantry have two most diabolical upward cuts, which we are too humane to use. Like this – three, four.'

'How murderous and bloodthirsty!'

'They are rather deathy. Now I'll be more interesting, and let you see some loose play – giving all the cuts and points, infantry and cavalry, quicker than lightning, and as promiscuously – with just enough rule to regulate instinct and yet not to fetter it. You are my antagonist, with this difference from real warfare, that I shall miss you every time by one hair's breadth, or perhaps two. Mind you don't flinch, whatever you do.'

'I'll be sure not to!' she said invincibly.

He pointed to about a yard in front of him.

Bathsheba's adventurous spirit was beginning to find some grains of relish in these highly novel proceedings. She took up her position as directed, facing Troy.

'Now, just to learn whether you have pluck enough to let me do what I wish, I'll give you a preliminary test.'

He flourished the sword by way of introduction number two, and the next thing of which she was conscious was that the point and blade of the sword were darting with a gleam towards her left side, just above her hip; then of their reappearance on her right side, emerging as it were from between her ribs, having apparently passed through her body. The third item of consciousness was that of seeing the same sword, perfectly clean and free from blood held vertically in Troy's hand (in the position technically called 'recover swords'). All was as quick as electricity.

'Oh!' She cried out in affright, pressing her hand to her side. 'Have you run me through? – no, you have not! Whatever have you done!'

'I have not touched you,' said Troy quietly. 'It was mere sleight of hand.'

(Chapter 28, 'The Hollow Amid the Ferns')

One of the most noteworthy aspects of this passage is the way in which it combines two entirely different kinds of discourse: the technical language of a highly specialized skill (swordsmanship), and the language of love, sex and seduction. On the one hand, there are such terms as 'cuts', 'points' and 'guards', which, since they were probably as unfamiliar to Bathsheba as they are to the modern reader, represent part of the mystique of Troy's occupation. (It is necessary to explain that the weapon used by Troy would have been the old-fashioned broadsword, with one sharp and one blunt edge, introduced into the British army in the eighteenth century. Cuts are hits made with the blunt edge of the sword; a point is a direct forward advance or charge with the sword; and guards are positions of defence adopted by the swordsman.)

In a term of swordsmanship such as 'thrusts', there is also an element of ambiguity and sexual innuendo that links the sword display – the *apparent* subject of the couple's attention and conversation – with its *real* subject, courtship and sexual display. Words such as 'instinct' and 'promiscuous' point clearly in the direction of the latter; more ambiguous, but unmistakably erotic in implication, are Troy's urging of Bathsheba 'to let me do what I wish', and the allusion to 'sowing . . . corn', a traditional metaphor for sexual intercourse. This last example suggests Troy's cunning as a practised seducer: to use the language of sowing and reaping seems perfectly natural in an agricultural community, but in this context the terms seem far from innocent.

On Bathsheba's side, there is a different kind of ambiguity, in that she is both terrified and fascinated by the sword and the combination of attraction, power and danger it represents. The weapon itself is unmistakably phallic (the narrator describes it as 'like a living thing'), and Troy seems well aware of its significance, and quite prepared to exploit his skill and to impress his companion. Even though, a little later, when Bathsheba exclaims that his performance is 'magic', he insists that he has employed no more than 'dexterity' ('sleight of hand' at the end of the passage above), he is in fact seeking to fascinate and bemuse, almost to hypnotize and bewitch her. He is successful in this aim, and there is great force in the narrator's observation that 'All was as quick as electricity', since the wonder of electricity was a much newer and more exciting idea to the Victorians than it is to ourselves.

At the same time, the narrator's reference to 'Bathsheba's adventurous spirit' reminds us that the scene develops the presentation of her character as well as the relationship between her and Troy: it is not every Victorian girl who would allow a young man to behave in this way, or would have the courage to stand firm in the face of what seems like a threat to life and limb. Troy, of course, encourages this by appealing to her 'pluck' and by turning the display into a challenge (he explicitly refers to 'a preliminary test').

Victorian middle-class courtship was conducted under strict rules of propriety, but Troy has discovered, and is exploiting to the full, a situation in which, without actually having physical contact with Bathsheba (which would probably be counterproductive), he can perform a kind of symbolic rape or seduction. The significance of the sword-play as a symbolic equivalent of a sexual act is most obvious in the paragraph that begins 'He flourished the sword...'. The rapid movements of Troy's sword create, for Bathsheba, the momentary illusion that she has been penetrated in various parts of her body – 'towards her left side', 'just above her hip', 'having apparently passed through her body'.

In this scene, and indeed throughout much of the novel, Bathsheba seems to be struggling a little uncertainly between two roles, one instinctive, the other imposed upon her by society, circumstance and conscience. As 'the mistress of the farm' – a role for which her earlier life has not prepared her – she is responsible for property and people: buildings, livestock, and the men and women who work for her. (The touching scene in the Corn Exchange stresses just how difficult a role this was for a young woman in this time and place.) But her instincts, not surprisingly, impel her not in the direction of becoming a representative of power and authority but to respond as a woman capable of love and passion. This is her dilemma throughout the novel, and there seems to be on Hardy's part an implied scepticism as to whether a 'female animal' (to use the blunt phrase he was much later to apply to Arabella in *Jude the Obscure*) can altogether suppress her instincts in obedience to social and economic imperatives.

From a coolly objective point of view, Bathsheba should be able to perceive that Troy would not make a satisfactory partner in the kind of life to which she has committed herself, while Gabriel Oak on the other hand is eminently fitted for that role. But her heart is stronger than her head, and there is no mistaking the force of the spell that Troy, with such apparent ease, exerts upon her, or the readiness with which she falls under that spell. If we compare this scene with the one in which Tess falls victim to the wiles of Alec, we can note both similarities and differences: Alec, like Troy, is evidently a practised seducer, but the social gap between him and Tess is greater than that between Troy and Bathsheba, and (partly perhaps as a result of this) Bathsheba has none of the gentleness, diffidence and passivity of Tess. The self-confidence and strength of character Bathsheba evinces in other areas of her life make all the more striking the rapidity with which she becomes physically attracted to and emotionally involved with Troy. But then the latter is in every way a more colourful character than Gabriel: the shepherd's drab working dress simply cannot compete with the soldier's scarlet uniform, and Bathsheba is too much at the mercy of her feelings to realize that it is a case of red for danger.

It needs to be stressed that this is, in a novel of the 1870s, a scene of extraordinary boldness. Almost throughout his career as a novelist, Hardy had problems with the kind of unofficial censorship exerted by publishers and editors, and some aspects of *Far from the Madding Crowd* were objected to and watered down when the novel was first published (see p. 25 above). It can only have been the pre-Freudian innocence of Hardy's contemporaries that allowed the scene in 'The Hollow Amid the Ferns' to get into print in a family magazine. To the modern reader, it is a remarkably intense account of a display of sexual power, whose participants are a man who believes himself to be irresistible and a woman who is both alarmed by the idea of male sexuality and fascinated by it.

The 'hollow' or natural hiding-place in which this scene occurs brings to mind significant locations in two other novels. We have seen that the young Jude Fawley, employed to scare the rooks away from Farmer Troutham's crop, feels himself imprisoned in a 'depression', a feature of the landscape that leaves the small boy surrounded by the horizon and the overarching sky. Somewhat differently, Bathsheba seems to have stepped voluntarily into a trap that she could leave at any time, were she not fascinated by Troy's presence. Michael Hench-ard is also trapped within a kind of hollow circular shape, this time the ancient monument of the Casterbridge 'Ring'; here, as with Jude, the physical environment seems to symbolize the way in which he is cut off from means of escape, and how his options in life are limited.

Psychoanalytic critics have gone further and also seen sexual symbolism in the setting of this episode: the description of the 'hollow' ('The pit was a saucer-shaped concave ... ') is both objectively precise ('with a top diameter of about thirty feet') and (to some interpreters) suggestive of the female body and genitalia. It also suggests an enclosed, claustrophobic world in which Bathsheba is temporarily imprisoned as a result of the spell Troy casts over her. In the structure of the story, the scene is important as leading to Bathsheba's eventual and disastrous marriage to Troy, but like many of Hardy's finest scenes it also seems to take place in a world from which, for the time being, everything else has been exlcuded and the attention of both characters and readers is focussed on what is happening before their eyes.

Jude the Obscure: Male Innocence and Female Designs

While the passage just discussed provides an example of male sexu-ality and domination, and of woman as the half-willing victim of a kind of symbolic or ritual seduction, we can turn to *Jude the Obscure* to find the gender roles reversed. What is now in question is male innocence and female experience. Early in that novel, the idealistic and unworldly Jude is shown as ardently pursuing his ambition to acquire learning and to enter the university. His intellectual development, remarkable enough, given his social and economic disadvantages, has left no time for lighter pursuits, and he is a sexual innocent. Then, in the passage that follows, he crosses the path of the sexually experienced Arabella, who – like Troy some twenty years earlier, but with a very different kind of weapon – proceeds to enact a symbolic seduction:

> And then he continued to dream, and thought he might become even a bishop by leading a pure, energetic, wise, Christian life. And what an example he would set! If his income were £5000 a year, he would give away £4500 in one form and another, and live sumptuously (for him) on the remainder. Well, on second thoughts, a bishop was absurd. He would draw the line at an archdeacon. Perhaps a man could be as good and as learned and as useful in the capacity of archdeacon as in that of bishop. Yet he thought of the bishop again.
>
> 'Meanwhile I will read, as soon as I am settled in Christminster, the books I have not been able to get hold of here: Livy, Tacitus, Herodotus, Aeschylus, Sophocles, Aristophanes –'
>
> 'Ha, ha, ha! Hoity-toity!' The sounds were expressed in light voices on the other side of the hedge, but he did not notice them. His thoughts went on:
>
> '– Euripides, Plato, Aristotle, Lucretius, Epictetus, Seneca, Antoninus. Then I must master other things: the Fathers thoroughly; Bede and ecclesiastical history generally; a smattering of Hebrew – I only know the letters as yet –'
>
> 'Hoity-toity!'
>
> '– but I can work hard. I have staying power in abundance, thank God! and it is that which tells.... Yes, Christminster shall be my Alma Mater, and I'll be her beloved son, in whom she shall be well pleased.'
>
> In his deep concentration on these transactions of the future Jude's walk had slackened, and he was now standing quite still, looking at the ground as though the future were thrown thereon by a magic lantern. On a sudden something smacked him sharply in the ear, and he

became aware that a soft cold substance had been flung at him, and had fallen at his feet.

A glance told him what it was – a piece of flesh, the characteristic part of a barrow-pig, which the countrymen used for greasing their boots, as it was useless for any other purpose. Pigs were rather plentiful hereabout, being bred and fattened in large numbers in certain parts of North Wessex.

On the other side of the hedge was a stream, whence, as he now for the first time realized, had come the slight sounds of voices and laughter that had mingled with his dreams. He mounted the bank and looked over the fence. On the further side of the stream stood a small homestead, having a garden and pigsties attached; in front of it, beside the brook, three young women were kneeling, with buckets and platters beside them containing heaps of pigs' chitterlings which they were washing in the running water. One or two pairs of eyes slyly glanced up, and perceiving that his attention had at last been attracted, and that he was watching them, they braced themselves for inspection by putting their mouths demurely into shape and recommencing their rinsing operations with assiduity.

'Thank you!' said Jude severely.

'I *didn't* throw it, I tell you!' asserted one girl to her neighbour, as if unconscious of the young man's presence.

'Nor I,' the second answered.

'O, Anny, how can you!' said the third.

'If I had thrown anything at all, it shouldn't have been *that*!'

'Pooh! I don't care for him!' And they laughed and continued their work, without looking up, still ostentatiously accusing each other.

Jude grew sarcastic as he wiped his face, and caught their remarks.

'*You* didn't do it – O no!' he said to the up-stream one of the three.

She whom he addressed was a fine dark-eyed girl, not exactly handsome, but capable of passing as such at a little distance, despite some coarseness of skin and fibre. She had a round and prominent bosom, full lips, perfect teeth, and the rich complexion of a Cochin hen's egg. She was a complete and substantial female animal – no more, no less; and Jude was almost certain that to her was attributable the enterprise of attracting his attention from dreams of the humaner letters to what was simmering in the minds around him.

(Part I, Chapter 6)

Visually and spatially, this passage has features in common with some of those already discussed – features that by now we have come to recognize as trademarks of Hardy's imagination and narrative method. Like Tess Durbeyfield, Michael Henchard, and so many others before him, Jude is walking along a road that is not only literally leading somewhere but is symbolically taking him into an as yet undetermined future. His mediatations precisely concern the nature of that future, but they are interrupted and dispersed by voices coming from within a kind of circle, an enclosed group occupied in a shared task. Initially this group is separated from Jude, who pursues his way 'on the other side of the hedge', and this seems to embody his desire to pursue the life-plan he has formulated and to shun worldly temptations that might distract him from the fulfilment of his schemes. Almost against his will, however, he is drawn into the circle as a result of the missile cheekily thrown by Arabella: it is as if, by reaching out of the group of nubile young women, she has drawn Jude into it and caused him to abandon the straight line he was pursuing. Somewhat like the 'hollow amid the ferns' in which Bathsheba feels the power of Troy's attractiveness in *Far from the Madding Crowd*, the place in which Arabella and her friends are working is an enclosed space bounded by the stream (another line that seems to compete with that of the road) and her father's homestead.

At the beginning of the passage the reader is given access to Jude's unspoken thoughts. His course of self-guided study and his ambition to become a scholar and a pillar of the Church have meant that girlfriends and marriage have so far had no part in his scheme of life. But all that is about to be dramatically changed, and the scene marks a turning-point in Jude's experience. The first paragraph quoted, though apparently narrative, conveys the flavour of Jude's reflections. Stylistically, the exclamation 'what an example...' and the colloquial 'Well, on second thoughts...' represent an invasion of the formal prose that is the normal medium for Hardy's narrative by a more informal, colloquial style that may be described as 'thought-speech'. This in turn modulates into direct speech (presentation of words actually 'spoken' by the character) – or, more precisely, into soliloquy, since Jude is thinking aloud or talking to himself.

It is an effective touch whereby Jude's sonorous muster-roll of ancient authors ('Livy, Tacitus...') is interrupted by a very different sound, that of the girls 'on the other side of the hedge'. This counter-pointing of Jude's learned catalogue with the cries and giggles of the girls makes a startling contrast and warns us that the young man is about to come into contact with a very different world from the one he is mentally inhabiting. At first he does not hear them: an incorri-gible idealist, he inhabits a world largely of his own imaginative creation, though it is about to be intruded upon by reality in a very tangible and solid form. The implication is that, caught up in the inner world of his dreams of learning, Jude is simply unaware of what is happening a few feet away.

The narrator sums up Jude's self-engrossed condition with the statement that Jude was 'looking at the ground as though the future were thrown thereon by a magic lantern'. This image is both char-acteristically Hardyan and strikingly modern, since a magic lantern, casting images on a screen, was a precursor of the cinema projector. Hardy's habit of visualization makes his hero not merely think about the future but *see* it: Jude sees vividly what is not literally there, just as later, when he arrives in Christminster, he sees not the living inhabit-ants of the town but the ghosts of dead writers and scholars. Persistently Jude is driven forward by an inner vision or dream that comes into violent collision with harsh reality, and this passage, early in the novel, is a prototype for much of what follows.

There is a nice example, too, of Hardy's subtle use of allusions to other texts – in this case, as so often, the Bible (which, for all his reputation as a godless man, he knew intimately). The phrase 'her beloved son, in whom she shall be well pleased' is quoted by Jude from St Matthew's Gospel (3:17), and in that context the reference is to Jesus Christ. This is just one of a number of references throughout the novel to Jude as a Christ-figure, doomed to suffer and die young. But his words, and his vision, are rudely interrupted by a sharp blow on the ear, and at this point Hardy introduces what may well be the most daring object to be found in any nineteenth-century novel openly published for a middle-class readership.

The girls are at work by a stream, washing parts of a pig that has recently been slaughtered (there is a reference to 'chitterlings', the intestines, that were cooked and eaten as a savoury dish). What one of the girls has thrown at Jude is referred to rather coyly as 'a piece of flesh, the characteristic part of a barrow-pig': in plain English, the animal's penis. The term 'barrow-pig', meaning a boar or male pig, would not be familiar to all Hardy's readers, and some no doubt would remain vague as to just what had been thrown; but the conversation that follows leaves the more sophisticated reader in no doubt that it has been a highly improper missile, and one intended to convey an unambiguous message.

This is Jude's introduction to Arabella, who is to play, intermittently, a large part in the novel until the very last sentence. We are left in no doubt that she and her companions are practised in the arts of enticing men: 'they braced themselves for inspection by putting their mouths demurely into shape'. Arabella naturally receives the closest attention from the narrator, and the description of her, though economical, is precise and vivid: the physical details – her dark eyes, 'full lips', 'perfect teeth', 'round and prominent bosom' – are combined with more general statements (she is 'capable of passing as [handsome] at a little distance'). Most striking of all is the summing-up of Arabella as 'a complete and substantial female animal – no more, no less...'. This prepares us for the role Arabella is to play in the thematic structure of the novel, as the opposite in nearly every respect of the 'intellectualized' Sue Bridehead.

The word 'animal', as applied to Arabella, also suggests a link with the subhuman world and the pig-killing in particular, and from this point onwards the association of Arabella, a butcher's daughter, with pigs is to be persistent. Perhaps Hardy has in mind the story, told by Homer in the *Odyssey*, of Circe the enchantress, who changed some of Odysseus's sailors into swine; but whether or not this mythological allusion is implicit, the linking of Arabella with pigs, and especially the brutal slaughtering of the animals for food, is prominent.

Hardy felt an immense compassion for the suffering inflicted by humans on animals, and took a strong interest in animal welfare organizations, which were remembered in his will. In his novels and poems there are many references both to the inhumanity of human beings in their treatment of wild and domesticated animals and to the violence and pain that is part of the natural order. Later in *Jude*, for instance, there is a powerful episode in which Jude and Arabella kill a pig they have reared themselves, and another scene in which Jude is troubled by the sufferings of a rabbit caught in a trap. This sensitivity and vulnerability on Jude's part are a handicap in the struggle for existence: things would be much easier for him if he shared Arabella's cheerful indifference. Furthermore, the pig imagery reinforces the idea that Jude is pulled down by his relationship with Arabella: repeatedly, his moral and intellectual aspirations are abandoned when he becomes involved with her, her sexual attractions (Hardy seems to suggest) reducing him to the level of an animal, or at least one motivated by instinct and appetite rather than reason.

The passage, occurring early in the novel, thus touches on a number of ideas and issues that will recur later. Jude's tendency to daydreaming and longing for the unattainable comes into sharp collision with the earthy reality of the sexually aware young women: in the last sentence quoted there is an ironic contrast between the formal and decorous reference to Jude's 'dreams of the humaner letters' and the word 'simmering' – a powerful metaphor for the strong and eager sexual desires felt by the working-class girls. The style of the passage effectively combines analysis and description with realistic dialogue. Thematically, the implication that an innocent young man has been set on the road to being seduced and betrayed by an experienced young woman reverses the traditional pattern of the male seducer and innocent female victim.

The Mayor of Casterbridge: Love and Rivalry

In the next passage, the situation is less obviously dramatic but more complex. It presents the relationship of a man with two different women, with a second man 'offstage' who is also an important element in the situation and indirectly makes an appearance. And whereas one of the women is experienced and articulate, the other is modest and reticent, so that what is taking place has to be presented to a large extent through analysis and commentary rather than action and dialogue. In this respect the passage exhibits a different novelistic technique from the two passages already considered in this chapter.

For the first time in their acquaintance Lucetta had the move; and yet she was backward. 'For the present let things be,' she said with some embarrassment. 'Treat me as an acquaintance, and I'll treat you as one. Time will –' She stopped; and he said nothing to fill the gap for awhile, there being no pressure of half acquaintance to drive them into speech if they were not minded for it.

'That's the way the wind blows, is it?' [Henchard] said at last grimly, nodding an affirmative to his own thoughts.

A yellow flood of reflected sunlight filled the room for a few instants. It was produced by the passing of a load of newly trussed hay from the country, in a waggon marked with Farfrae's name. Beside it rode Farfrae himself on horseback. Lucetta's face became – as a woman's face becomes when the man she loves rises upon her gaze like an apparition.

A turn of the eye by Henchard, a glance from the window, and the secret of her inaccessibility would have been revealed. But Henchard in estimating her tone was looking down so plumb-straight that he did not note the warm consciousness upon Lucetta's face.

'I shouldn't have thought it – I shouldn't have thought it of women!' he said emphatically by-and-by, rising and shaking himself into activity; while Lucetta was so anxious to divert him from any suspicion of the truth that she asked him to be in no hurry. Bringing him some apples she insisted upon paring one for him.

He would not take it. 'No, no; such is not for me,' he said drily, and moved to the door. At going out he turned his eye upon her.

'You came to live in Casterbridge entirely on my account,' he said. 'Yet now you are here you won't have anything to say to my offer!'

He had hardly gone down the staircase when she dropped upon the sofa and jumped up again in a fit of desperation. 'I *will* love him!' she cried passionately; 'as for *him* – he's hot-tempered and stern, and it would be madness to bind myself to him knowing that. I won't be a slave to the past – I'll love where I choose!'

Yet having decided to break away from Henchard one might have supposed her capable of aiming higher than Farfrae. But Lucetta reasoned nothing: she feared hard words from the people with whom she had been earlier associated; she had no relatives left; and with native lightness of heart took kindly to what fate offered.

Elizabeth-Jane, surveying the position of Lucetta between her two lovers from the crystalline sphere of a straightforward mind, did not fail to perceive that her father, as she called him, and Donald Farfrae became more desperately enamoured of her friend every day. On Farfrae's side it was the unforced passion of youth. On Henchard's the artificially stimulated coveting of maturer age.

The pain she experienced from the almost absolute obliviousness to her existence that was shown by the pair of them became at times half dissipated by her sense of its humorousness. When Lucetta had pricked her finger they were as deeply concerned as if she were dying; when she herself had been seriously sick or in danger they uttered a conventional word of sympathy at the news, and forgot all about it immediately. But, as regarded Henchard, this perception of hers also caused her some filial grief; she could not help asking what she had done to be neglected so, after the professions of solicitude he had made. As regarded Farfrae, she thought, after honest reflection, that it was quite natural. What was she beside Lucetta? – as one of the 'meaner beauties of the night', when the moon had risen in the skies.

She had learnt the lesson of renunciation, and was as familiar with the wreck of each day's wishes as with the diurnal setting of the sun. If her earthly career had taught her few book philosophies it had at least well practised her in this. Yet her experience had consisted less in a series of pure disappointments than in a series of substitutions. Continually it had happened that what she had desired had not been granted her, and that what had been granted her she had not desired. So she viewed with an approach to equanimity the now cancelled days when Donald had been her undeclared lover, and wondered what unwished-for thing Heaven might send her in place of him.

(Chapter 25)

The passage analyses and dramatizes the complex relationships that exist between two men and two women. Henchard, who has had an affair with Lucetta while she was still in Jersey, now wishes to marry her – both because he is lonely and because doing so will ease his conscience and guarantee his respectability in the eyes of the community. But Lucetta no longer cares for him, having fallen in love with Donald Farfrae, who returns her love. While Lucetta is the object of the attentions of both men, however, Elizabeth-Jane is neglected by both, and her intense feelings find no expression in words or action. She cannot understand why Henchard, who at first seemed to show real affection for her, now displays only indifference (the reader, of course, is aware that Henchard has learned that she is not really his child); and her romantic feelings for Farfrae are utterly unrecognized by the young Scot.

The first part of the passage dramatizes Lucetta's situation in a way that is very characteristic of Hardy's fictional use of space. (Comparison may be made with another passage from the same novel discussed in Chapter 4: see pp. 100–5 above.) The interview between Henchard and Lucetta takes place indoors, but the house is situated in the middle of Casterbridge, and the window of the room overlooks a busy street. As they talk, a hay-cart with Farfrae's name painted on it, accompanied by Farfrae himself on horseback, passes beneath the window and is seen by Lucetta, though not by Henchard, while Farfrae himself is unaware that he is the object of Lucetta's close and excited attention.

This motif of watching or spying is frequently used by Hardy, and is here complicated by Henchard's failure to observe what is happening a few yards away – one of many failures on his part to grasp a fact or situation in a way that might enable him to behave more wisely. Also very characteristic is the pictorial touch that lends vividness to the passing of Farfrae and his cart: Hardy does not simply tell us that they passed by, but makes us *see* the room suddenly and briefly illuminated by a 'yellow flood of reflected sunlight'. Like the Impressionist painters who were working at about the time this novel was written, and with whose work he became familiar, Hardy was fond of what he called 'chromatic' effects (compare the use of the colour red in *Tess*), and the sudden 'flooding' of the room by the colour of the load of hay makes Farfrae's silent presence felt, almost bringing him into the room. Since he and Henchard become rivals in the hay and corn trade as well as rivals for Lucetta's love, the point made here is a particularly strong one, and it is interesting that it is made not through commentary or speech but through a vivid visual instant.

The economical dialogue marks the contrast between Henchard and Lucetta. The former is a man of action rather than speech, and is uncomfortable with language; in this respect, as in many others, he stands in contrast to Farfrae. His manner is brusque and peremptory (Lucetta is justified in describing him as 'hot-tempered and stern'), for he cannot understand why she should be unwilling to marry him – and this is indeed another failure on his part, this time not of observation but of sensitivity and awareness of the possible feelings of another person. Her manner, on the other hand, is evasive: she does not wish to precipitate a crisis, but she is unwilling to commit herself to Henchard, and after he has gone her short soliloquy is a kind of declaration of independence: 'I'll love where I choose!' But in Victorian bourgeois society a woman ran risks in making such a declaration, and the workings-out of the plot later demonstrate that her sacrifice of prudence to passion involves paying a price. (After her marriage to Farfrae, her former liaison with Henchard becomes public knowledge and indirectly leads to her death.)

Lucetta's character, with its tendency to allow her to be carried away by her feelings into doing something against her worldly inter-ests, is highlighted by contrast with that of Elizabeth-Jane. The latter is, throughout the novel, unusually silent for a major character – though, as it turns out, the final words of the novel are devoted to her, and there is good reason for supposing that she represents a type of personality that Hardy found deeply interesting and with which he to some extent identified. She possesses, according to the narrator, a 'straightforward mind', observing in a more or less detached manner the wayward behaviour and turbulent emotions of others.

Though not without strong feelings herself, Elizabeth-Jane is capable of keeping them under control. Her father's neglect and indifference cause her 'pain', but she can also see the ludicrous side of the infatuation felt by these two men for Lucetta; her stance, in other words, is a complex mixture of involvement and detach-ment. As for Farfrae, it seems to her 'quite natural' that he should prefer the sophisticated and fashionable Lucetta. This modesty, amounting to self-disparagement, and this absence of protest or complaint are summed up by the narrator: 'She had learnt the lesson of renunciation...', and the lines that follow, with the touch-ing metaphor of 'the wreck of each day's wishes', place her present feelings in the context of her life as a whole. Her aim in life, it seems, is not so much passion or intense experience as 'an approach to equanimity'. (Significantly, this last word is used by Hardy in a very personal poem written in the 1890s, 'I Look into My Glass').

It is worth noting that there is in Elizabeth-Jane's situation at this point in the story an element of dramatic irony, a term used especially in relation to the drama of Ancient Greece (with which Hardy was well acquainted) and referring to the contrast between a character's ignorance of some important fact and the audience's knowledge of it. Here, the reader knows, as the girl does not, that Henchard's attitude towards her has undergone a profound change as a result of his reading the letter left by his dead wife.

A point of narrative technique in this passage is that the first half uses mainly dialogue and revealing action (such as Henchard's blunt refusal of the apples Lucetta offers him), whereas the second half consists entirely of commentary and analysis. Another way of putting this would be to suggest that the scene between Lucetta and Henchard, like those considered earlier in this chapter that take place between Bathsheba and Troy and between Jude and Arabella, would lend themselves readily to dramatization. In contrast, the section that concerns Elizabeth-Jane (which is not a 'scene' at all) is more essentially literary and novelistic in nature. We do not hear Elizabeth-Jane's 'voice' for the simple reason that there is no-one, since her mother's death, in whom she can confide: the woman she knows best is Lucetta, and ironically Lucetta is precisely the one woman to whom she cannot speak about her feelings, even if it had been in her nature to do so.

Tess of the d'Urbervilles: Ideal and Reality in Love

The following pivotal scene takes place on the wedding night of Tess and Angel. His confession, readily forgiven by Tess, of a premarital liaison is followed by her own confession of her past relationship with Alec. The contrast in their reactions to this mutual truth-telling provides an insight into the radical difference in their characters, and Angel's refusal to forgive Tess also exemplifies the 'double standard' that operated so widely, in Victorian society and literature, in relation to the sexual lives and feelings of women.

Her narrative ended; even its re-assertions and secondary explanations were done. Tess's voice throughout had hardly risen higher than its opening tone; there had been no exculpatory phrase of any kind, and she had not wept.

But the complexion even of external things seemed to suffer transmutation as her announcement progressed. The fire in the grate looked impish – demoniacally funny, as if it did not care in the least about her strait. The fender grinned idly, as if it too did not care. The light from the water-bottle was merely engaged in a chromatic problem. All material objects around announced their irresponsibility with terrible iteration. And yet nothing had changed since the moments when he had been kissing her; or rather, nothing in the substance of things. But the essence of things had changed.

When she ceased the auricular impressions from their previous endearments seemed to hustle away into the corners of their brains, repeating themselves as echoes from a time of supremely purblind foolishness.

Clare performed the irrelevant act of stirring the fire; the intelligence had not even yet got to the bottom of him. After stirring the embers he rose to his feet; all the force of her disclosure had imparted itself now. His face had withered. In the strenuousness of his concentration he treadled fitfully on the floor. He could not, by any contrivance, think clearly enough; that was the meaning of his vague movement. When he spoke it was in the most inadequate, commonplace voice of the many varied tones she had heard from him.

'Tess!'

'Yes, dearest.'

'Am I to believe this? From your manner I am to take it as true. O you cannot be out of your mind! You ought to be! Yet you are not. . . . My wife, my Tess – nothing in you warrants such a supposition as that?'

'I am not out of my mind,' she said.

'And yet –' He looked vacantly at her, to resume with dazed senses: 'Why didn't you tell me before? Ah, yes, you would have told me, in a way – but I hindered you, I remember!'

These and other of his words were nothing but the perfunctory babble of the surface while the depths remained paralysed. He turned away, and bent over a chair. Tess followed him to the middle of the room where he was, and stood there staring at him with eyes that did not weep. Presently she slid down upon her knees beside his foot, and from this position she crouched in a heap.

'In the name of our love, forgive me!' she whispered with a dry mouth. 'I have forgiven you for the same!'

And, as he did not answer, she said again –

'Forgive me as you are forgiven! *I* forgive *you*, Angel.'

'You – yes, you do.'

'But you do not forgive me?'

'O Tess, forgiveness does not apply to the case! You were one person; now you are another. My God – how can forgiveness meet such a grotesque – prestidigitation as that!'

He paused, contemplating this definition; then suddenly broke into horrible laughter – as unnatural and ghastly as a laugh in hell.

'Don't – don't! It kills me quite, that!' she shrieked. 'O have mercy upon me – have mercy!'

He did not answer; and, sickly white, she jumped up.

'Angel, Angel! what do you mean by that laugh?' she cried out. 'Do you know what this is to me?'

He shook his head.

'I have been hoping, longing, praying, to make you happy! I have thought what joy it will be to do it, what an unworthy wife I shall be if I do not! That's what I have felt, Angel!'

'I know that.'

'I thought, Angel, that you loved me – me, my very self! If it is I you do love, O how can it be that you look and speak so? It frightens me! Having begun to love you, I love you for ever – in all changes, in all disgraces, because you are yourself. I ask no more. Then how can you, O my own husband, stop loving me?'

'I repeat, the woman I have been loving is not you.'

'But who?'

'Another woman in your shape.'

She perceived in his words the realization of her own apprehensive foreboding in former times. He looked upon her as a species of impostor; a guilty woman in the guise of an innocent one. Terror was upon her white face as she saw it; her cheek was flaccid, and her mouth had almost the aspect of a round little hole. The horrible sense of his view of her so deadened her that she staggered; and he stepped forward, thinking she was going to fall.

'Sit down, sit down,' he said gently. 'You are ill; and it is natural that you should be.'

(Chapter 35)

This passage appears at the very beginning of 'Phase the Fifth' of Hardy's novel, which bears the title 'The Woman Pays', and it forms one of the major turning-points of the story. Tess and Angel have just been married, bringing to a culmination the long development of their love for each other during the idyllic period spent at Talbothays Farm. In the evening Tess decides to do what she had long intended to do but had lacked courage: to tell Angel about her affair with Alec and and the baby she has borne and lost. The previous chapter, and the fourth 'phase' of Tess's story, has ended with her 'murmuring the words' to Angel, and the opening paragraph of the extract above contains an echo of this description.

The paragraph that follows is essentially Hardyan. Hardy sometimes used the term 'idiosyncratic' in speaking of his own individual vision or perception of external reality, and there is certainly something unexpected, even eccentric, and highly personal about the means he uses to convey the effect of Tess's narrative. Most novelists, perhaps, would at this point find some means, dramatic or otherwise, of demonstrating the emotions of the couple, and especially of Angel. But Angel is not even mentioned by name, and Tess herself has 'not wept' and apparently registers no outward sign of change. Paradoxically, it is to the inanimate objects in the room – commonplace material things like the fender and the water-bottle – that attention is now directed.

It is not immediately obvious whether the change in 'the complexion...of external things' is perceived by either or both of the characters present or is part of the narrator's objective commentary on the situation. Even though Angel is not mentioned by name, however, the pronoun 'he' in the penultimate sentence of the paragraph clearly refers to him, just as the reference to 'her strait' in the second sentence applies to Tess. It is possible that it is the two of them who are overcome by a powerful sense that the external world has undergone a profound change – to whom the grate and fender appear to be taking a malicious pleasure in the situation, and the water-bottle is showing its indifference by being absorbed in 'a chromatic problem'. (In this last phrase Hardy is thinking, as an Impressionist painter might, of the way in which a ray of light, presumably from the fire, plays upon a glass vessel containing water.) But the point cannot be proved, and there seems to be a genuine ambiguity. What is undoubtedly true is that the narrative mode at this point is poetic and philosophical rather than realistic: the fanciful references to inanimate objects offer one example of a favourite Hardyan idea, that subjective feelings can have the effect of transforming the perceived appearance of the external world.

The important point is, however, that the external world seems to be demonstrating its 'irresponsibility' and indifference: the world does not collapse, however devastating human emotions may be. As the epigrammatic conclusion to this paragraph puts it, the change is in 'essence' not 'substance'. The language is philosophical, and indeed the ideas pursued in this paragraph seem to belong to the spheres of philosophy and psychology. There is an acute psychological touch a little later when Angel's poking the fire is described as an 'irrelevant act'. The fire does not need poking, but the simple physical task offers some slight relief from his burden of feelings: a relief that he does not yet feel able to find in verbal expression. Equally acute is the observation that when he does speak it is in a 'commonplace voice'. Hardy is resisting here the temptation to exploit the situation and give the reader a scene of high drama or melodrama. There is much greater psychological realism in his depiction of Angel's behaviour: whatever novels and dramas may often suggest, in moments of real crisis people do not always, or often, rise to great eloquence.

The rest of the passage, in contrast to what has preceded it, consists mainly of dialogue and the accompaniments of dialogue – including, for example, Angel's 'horrible laughter' and such descriptive verbs as 'whispered' and 'shrieked'. The scene is conceived in dramatic terms, and it is easy to see why the novel was so readily and successfully adapted for the stage (and later the cinema). Of particular note is the paragraph beginning 'These and other of his words...', which shows the movements and postures of the two actors in the scene, very much in the manner of stage-directions in a dramatic script. At the end of the paragraph Tess has sunk into an attitude that traditionally symbolizes contrition and submission, indicating her admission of guilt and her plea for forgiveness and mercy.

And yet this is not really an accurate assessment of the situation in its moral sense, for Tess has been less a sinner than one sinned against – the victim of an unscrupulous seducer who has not only physical strength but knowledge of the world and the power derived from wealth and social status on his side. In moral terms the most striking aspect of the scene is that Angel completely fails to recognize this. He is so absorbed by his own feelings, and especially by the collapse of his idealized and romantic conception of Tess as a virginal 'child of nature', that he has no understanding of her situation and no real feeling for the woman he claims to love.

We know from earlier passages in the novel that Angel has reacted against his very conventional Christian upbringing and aspires to liberal and enlightened opinions. Put to the test, however, as he now is, he shows himself to be utterly conventional in accepting without question the 'double standard' whereby a woman is condemned for moral offences that are regarded as relatively trivial in a man. When Tess, with good reason, protests that she deserves forgiveness because 'I have forgiven you for the same!', he does not reply, for the reason that he does not accept that their respective offences are 'the same'. Tess, in her artless way, goes unerringly to the core of the matter when she beseeches him, 'Forgive me as you are forgiven!' The reference is to the confession made by Angel a little earlier of a moral lapse, for which Tess has unhesitatingly declared her forgiveness. Yet he is unwilling to recognize that their situations are parallel, insisting that 'forgiveness does not apply to the case!'

What does Angel mean by 'the case'? He answers his question himself when he declares, 'You were one person; now you are another.' Against this, a few lines later, Tess pathetically sets her belief that he had loved 'my very self', but his only response is to insist that 'the woman I have been loving is not you'. Unconsciously, Angel betrays the limitations and defects of his own kind of loving:

he has been in love with an idea, not a woman, and the reader is left in no doubt that Tess's kind of love ('for ever') is immeasurably superior to his. Angel is the better educated of the two and is sometimes patronizing and insensitive in his attitude to Tess (he must be aware that his pedantic phrase 'grotesque – prestidigitation' is likely to mean nothing to her), but she has the finer nature. The difference between them is that whereas Angel's convictions are intellectual in origin, probably nourished partly by his reading of romantic literature, Tess's are instinctive, springing from the genuine and spontaneous impulses of her nature.

The closing lines of this powerful extract are again dramatic in their depiction of violent emotion and in the contrast between the reactions of the two characters. The sentence beginning 'Terror...' gives a sharp visual sense of the way in which the human face can be transformed by extreme feelings, and the word 'staggered' indicates that what has taken place has had an effect upon Tess's whole body. Angel, on the other hand, speaks in a collected, rather formal way – evidence that his own emotions have been much less powerfully affected, and suggesting that what has been damaged by Tess's revelation is an intellectual idea rather than his deepest feelings. The scene therefore makes an important contribution to the characterization of Angel, as well as helping to determine the tragic future course of Tess's history.

Conclusions

In this chapter we have examined passages that exemplify Hardy's presentation of different aspects of male–female relationships inside and outside marriage. The extraordinary courtship ritual, amounting to symbolic seduction, represented by Troy's display of expert swordsmanship to Bathsheba exhibits aggressive male sexuality and the desire for domination; on the woman's part there is a mixture of fear and fascination. In contrast, Arabella's outrageous missile thrown at the innocent Jude is an unmistakable invitation to a sexual relationship on the part of a calculating and predatory woman who is prepared to make very conscious use of her physical attractions in order to ensnare a partner in marriage. Implicit in this situation is a social, economic and legal system that requires a woman to find a husband or face a probably unpleasant alternative. In this respect there is an important difference between the two women: Arabella lives in her parents' home and her economic prospects are uncertain, but Bathsheba very early in the story finds herself a woman of independent means and therefore at liberty to choose a mate regardless of worldly considerations – or indeed not to choose a mate if that is her wish.

The passage from *The Mayor of Casterbridge* explores a more complex network of relationships between four persons. Henchard and Farfrae are rivals for Lucetta; Lucetta has loved Henchard in the past but has now transferred her feelings to the younger man; Elizabeth-Jane has feelings of affection towards Henchard, whom she wrongly believes to be her father, and more romantic feelings towards Farfrae, who has earlier encouraged her but has now fallen under Lucetta's spell. The quartet thus represent a range of feelings, sexual and otherwise. Questions of class and status are at issue (Lucetta, though morally inferior to Elizabeth-Jane, is her social superior), and there is also a generational aspect, Henchard being a much older man than Farfrae. Again there is a notable contrast between the economic status of the two women: Lucetta's advantages of birth and education are reinforced by her status as a woman of independent means, whereas Elizabeth-Jane's status is the precarious one of a dependant upon Henchard.

Finally, Tess's revelation and Angel's reaction to it destroy the marriage that has hardly begun, the scene forming a turning-point in Tess's fortunes. All the odds are now stacked against the woman: in background and education as well as social and economic status, Tess is at a disadvantage compared with her husband, and it is significant that, after they part, he has the freedom to go anywhere in the world (he decides to emigrate to Brazil), whereas her only option is to take employment at a farm in another part of Wessex.

Repeatedly, in his presentation of love and sex, Hardy demonstrates that his characters – and by implication humanity in general – are not free to make choices but find themselves under the control of a variety of forces, biological, social, moral and religious. Bathsheba's freedom and independence, which she has vigorously defended in a male-dominated society, are jeopardized by her instinctive response to Troy's ostentatious sexuality, just as Jude's serious life-plan is sabotaged by Arabella's calculated appeal to his suppressed desires. In both cases biological instincts, which Hardy would have seen in Darwinian terms as the powerful urge of the species to perpetuate its kind, prove stronger than conscious and rational wishes and decisions.

Lucetta's transference of feeling from her old lover, Henchard, to the new one, Farfrae, is also instinctive, though here more stress is laid on emotions and sentiments than on physical desire. 'Lucetta reasoned nothing,' Hardy tells us, and indeed a sober assessment of the situation might have told her that she was making trouble for herself in the small community in which she has chosen to settle. It is difficult to believe that Hardy means us to take Lucetta's feelings very seriously, and her volatility is contrasted with the steadfastness of Elizabeth-Jane. (It is significant that, later in the novel, the one is rather summarily dispatched while the other remains a moral presence until the very last words of the text.) The point is, though, that once again a character is shown as out of control in relation to her/his romantic and sexual existence.

Tess and Angel have responded to biological urges during their idyllic courtship period at Talbothays, but the failure of their marriage stems from quite different causes. The irony of Angel's situation is that, while believing himself to be a man of progressive and enlightened ideas, he is thoroughly conventional in his views on women and his embracing of a double standard of conduct whereby the sexual transgressions of men are viewed more tolerantly. His insistence that the Tess he loved, or thought he loved, does not really exist has its origins in a moral code taught by his upbringing and education (we see enough of his parent and brothers to understand this). Though the cause may be different, however, the result is the same: human beings are shown as at the mercy of forces which, whether inside or outside themselves, are beyond their conscious and rational control.

Methods of Analysis

A major consideration in this chapter has been how far Hardy uses dramatic methods in presenting scenes of this kind, and how far the dramatic elements are reinforced and supplemented by other elements that are distinctively literary or novelistic – in other words, that would not so readily have a counterpart in a dramatic version of the scene produced in the theatre or cinema. Speech and body language are of primary importance in the episode from *Far from the Madding Crowd*, but the narrative also brings out the symbolic nature of the setting in the 'hollow amid the ferns'. The scene from *Jude* seems to approximate quite closely to a dramatic script, though there is the occasional intrusion of narratorial commentary (for example, to explain, somewhat coyly, the nature of Arabella's missile). Notable here is the use of space, with Jude at first on the other side of the hedge and mentally in a world of his own, then drawing closer (in more senses than one) to the girls by the stream.

Space is also exploited skilfully in the scene from *The Mayor of Casterbridge*, where the reader is given a strong sense of indoor and outdoor locations and of the placing of characters in relation to each other. The excerpt from *Tess* is the one that most clearly makes uses of non-dramatic elements: the second paragraph, for instance, has something of the quality of a prose-poem dropped into the text, and could hardly be reproduced in a dramatized version of the scene. At the same time, once the narrative mode switches to dialogue, we are given a very vivid sense of such dramatic elements as facial expression, tone of voice, movement and posture.

Suggestions for Further Work

Questions of love, sex and marriage are so integral to Hardy's fiction that almost any of his novels will provide abundant material for examination. To select instances almost at random, you may like to look at the following:

1. The second half of Chapter 4 of *Far from the Madding Crowd* (from 'When Gabriel had gone about two hundred yards...'), in which Gabriel proposes to, and is refused by, Bathsheba. Given Gabriel's unassertive nature, this makes an interesting contrast with the scene involving Bathsheba and Troy discussed above.

2. Chapter 29 of *The Mayor of Casterbridge*, from the beginning to '...as ungenerous as it was unwise'. This describes an encounter between Lucetta, Elizabeth-Jane and a bull, from which they are rescued by Henchard.

3. Chapter 5 of *Tess of the d'Urbervilles*, from 'Tess still stood hesitating...', which narrates the heroine's first meeting with Alec.

4. *Jude the Obscure*, Part VI, Chapter 8, from 'A light footstep...' to '...Jude did as she requested'. This tormented scene describes Jude's last meeting with Sue and her rejection of his love.

PART 2

THE CONTEXT

7

Hardy's Life and Work

Hardy had three careers – as architect, novelist and poet – and they overlapped and have a complex and interesting relationship to each other. Far from robust as a child, he received relatively little formal education. At eight years old he was sent to the village school, but soon afterwards his mother, an energetic woman ambitious for her firstborn, moved him to a school in the nearby town of Dorchester, where he would be able to study Latin under a good teacher. At sixteen he left school, and though he later suggested that it might have been possible for him to have gone to university at the age of twenty-five, that was the end of his formal education.

He remained, however, a lifelong student with a keen appetite for a wide range of knowledge, and during his youth he embarked on an ambitious and extensive programme of self-education. He himself said of this period of his life that it was composed of three strands: his daily work in an architect's office in Dorchester, where he had begun to serve an apprenticeship on leaving school; his home life in the rural community; and his arduous study of Greek and Latin, literature, history and theology.

In social terms, Hardy's origins were modest. He was the first of the four children of Thomas and Jemima Hardy: the former, like his own father before him, was a builder and stonemason, while his mother had been a servant before her marriage. Hardy's birthplace, which now belongs to the National Trust and is visited every year by thousands of fans from all over the world, was situated in the tiny hamlet of Upper Bockhampton, in the parish of Stinsford. This consisted of little more than a few homes at the end of a lane leading nowhere in particular, on the edge of the wild area (much wilder in Hardy's time than it is today) that he refers to as Egdon Heath. But the busy market town, and county town, of Dorchester was only three miles away, and he must have become aware very early in his life of the contrast of town and country. (*The Mayor of Casterbridge* contains his fullest depiction of Dorchester life and the intimate relationship of the urban community to the surrounding country-side.)

As a child Hardy became for a time the object of attention of the local lady of the manor, Mrs Julia Augusta Martin. She obviously recognized his exceptional abilities and took an interest in his educa-tion, and for his part the sensitive, intelligent child was fascinated by her wealth, elegance and sophistication. To this early experience can possibly be traced his obsession with the theme of 'the poor man and the lady' – a phrase he used as the title of his first novel (never published and later destroyed), and a recurring preoccupation in much of his fiction.

Later he was encouraged by Horace Moule, the Cambridge-edu-cated son of a local vicar, with whom Hardy formed a close friend-ship; Moule was a depressive personality, however, and his suicide in 1873 made a deep impression on Hardy. Such relationships as those with Mrs Martin and Horace Moule must have sharpened the young Hardy's awareness of social differences and made him highly sensit-ive to his own humble origins. Though he later achieved fame and riches, and built himself a large and imposing house on the outskirts of Dorchester, this sensitivity remained acute, and class differences remain one of the most striking features of his fiction. Very often, for instance, a love-relationship will be complicated, as in *Tess of the d'Urbervilles*, by disparities of social and economic status.

At 22 Hardy moved to London and worked there for a leading architect, specializing in the 'restoration' or rebuilding of ancient churches that had fallen into decay and disrepair. (See p. 116 above for a reference to this in *Jude the Obscure*.) He had begun writing poetry in his teens, and his earliest surviving poem – a description in Wordsworthian blank verse of the cottage, built by his grandfather, in which he was born – was written before he was twenty. In London he continued to write poems, some of them referring to an unhappy love affair of this period. When he submitted his work to magazines, however, it was wholly without success. We can now see that his highly individual style and his metrical experiments, in many ways at odds with mainstream Victorian verse, must have seemed awkward and unfamiliar to editors. But Hardy's disappointment was evident, and, though he continued to write poems, he was nearly sixty before he published a volume of verse.

In the age of Dickens and George Eliot, both of whom had come from humble origins and been hugely successful as writers, it was clear that anyone who wished to become a professional author would do well to turn to the novel, and in his late twenties Hardy's literary ambitions took that direction. Over the next quarter of a century he was to produce a steady stream of novels and short stories: the final count was fourteen published novels and about forty stories. Towards the end of that period, especially with the considerable success of *Tess of the d'Urbervilles*, fiction-writing brought him wealth and fame. He was often inclined to insist that this career as a novelist was not one he would have chosen, and it is perfectly true that poetry was his first love. But his protestations that his ambition as a novelist was, as he told one of his early editors, merely to be regarded as 'a good hand at a serial' need not be taken too literally. Long after he abandoned the art of fiction he went on scrupulously revising the texts of his novels for republication, and giving this kind of close attention to his texts does not sound like the action of a man who was cynically and opportunistically producing fiction as a commodity to satisfy the demands of the market.

At the outset his career as a novelist involved two or three false starts, and one has the distinct impression of a lack on Hardy's part of definite direction or a strong sense of what kind of novel he wanted to write. *The Poor Man and the Lady*, already mentioned, was evidently a radical social satire expressive of the young writer's aggrieved sense of the stifling class-consciousness of English society. Advised to avoid this kind of polemical novel and to produce a work with stronger plotting, he carried the advice to extremes, and his first published novel, *Desperate Remedies* (1871), which appeared at his own expense, was a conscious exercise in the 'sensation novel' that had

been immensely popular in the 1860s. Full of melodrama, it nevertheless has some unmistakably individual touches. Then, in complete
contrast, he produced a short love story, *Under the Greenwood Tree*
(1872), which draws on his intimate knowledge of country life,
speech and customs. Modest in scope, this is a complete success
and already contains themes and situations that were to recur in his
later fiction – for example, the fickle heroine who has to choose
between suitors of varying social status.

In the event he was to define himself as a historian or 'chronicler'
of rural life, and his greatest achievement in fiction, in the master-
pieces of his later phase, was to combine the pastoral novel both with
social criticism and with the grander aspirations of tragedy. As a
writer of pastoral he was greatly influenced by George Eliot (1819–
80), who, a few years before Hardy turned to the novel, had demonstrated in such works as *Adam Bede* (1859) and *Silas Marner* (1861) that
the rural novel was wholly compatible with a serious concern with
psychological and moral issues.

Traditionally, the pastoral mode celebrates the peace and innocence of country life ('pastoral' literally means 'concerning shepherds'), and it has usually been linked with the idea of escapism,
especially the flight from urban life and its cares and responsibilities.
There is, however, little that is idyllic or idealizing about Hardy's
version of pastoral. *Far from the Madding Crowd* has (like *Under the
Greenwood Tree*) one of the poetic titles fashionable at the time, but a
comparison of the source – Thomas Gray's 'Elegy Written in a
Country Churchyard', perhaps the most famous English poem of
the eighteenth century (see also p. 26 above) – with the novel exposes
Hardy's use of the phrase as ironic. There is nothing 'sequestered' or
sheltered from the world about the lives of the major characters in
this novel, and the action includes suffering and death, murder and
madness.

It is in that same novel that Hardy first refers to the ancient Saxon
kingdom of Wessex. He was to adopt this term, previously familiar
mainly to students of history, as a name for the territory of his own
fictions, which covers a large part of south-west England. Even so,
he did not quickly or easily assume the role of historian of rural life.
Though his rural characters earned praise from early reviewers, he

was clearly reluctant to become typecast as a 'provincial' writer, and between his two major novels *The Return of the Native* (1878) and *The Mayor of Casterbridge* (1886) he published three lesser novels that belong to different subgenres from the pastoral: *The Trumpet-Major* (1880), a historical novel dealing with the Napoleonic period; *A Laodicean* (1881), a novel of middle-and upper-class life with an architectural theme; and *Two on a Tower* (1882), a romance about an affair between a young astronomer and an aristocratic lady (yet another reworking of the 'poor man and the lady' motif).

With *The Mayor of Casterbridge*, however, Hardy returned to the scenes of his own early life, and this work inaugurates the series of great tragic novels that ends with *Jude the Obscure*. In these works Hardy infuses the novel of more-or-less contemporary life with elements derived from classical and Shakespearean tragedy, so that the confined world of 'Wessex' takes on a universal resonance. In *The Mayor*, for instance, Michael Henchard has much in common with Shakespeare's King Lear, and the reference to the Greek tragic dramatist Aeschylus on the last page of *Tess* is no accident.

To return to the progress of Hardy's early career as a novelist: his first commercial success came with his fourth published novel, *Far from the Madding Crowd* (1874), which appeared originally in twelve monthly instalments in the prestigious *Cornhill Magazine*. On the strength of this success Hardy took two important steps: he abandoned architecture in order to become a full-time writer, and he married a young woman called Emma Gifford, whom he had met a few years earlier while engaged on architectural business in Cornwall. This marriage was to last until Emma's death in 1912, and the considerable strains to which it was subjected help to account for the major role played by questions of marriage and divorce in Hardy's later fiction (most notably in his last novel, *Jude the Obscure*).

From an early stage, though not from the very beginning, Hardy's novels appeared as serials in newspapers or magazines, usually in both England and America, before appearing in volume form. This mode of double publication, with two different sources of profit for the author, had been established, with resounding success, by Dickens and had been followed by most of the major Victorian novelists, including Thackeray, Trollope and George Eliot. It survived until the end of the century, and it perhaps comes as a surprise to find that a modernist masterpiece such as Joseph Conrad's *Heart of Darkness* was originally serialized in 1899 in an Edinburgh magazine.

Serial publication had significant structural effects on a work of fiction, since each instalment was expected to contain a certain amount of action, and this tended to generate a heavily plotted novel. It also encouraged the type of fiction that deals with secrets and mysteries, which would naturally tend to encourage readers to go on buying the publication. Hardy himself felt that such influences could come into conflict with more strictly artistic aims: he later remarked of *The Mayor of Casterbridge*, for instance, that 'It was a story which [he] fancied he had damaged more recklessly as an artistic whole, in the interest of the newspaper in which it appeared serially, than perhaps any other of his novels, his aiming to get an incident into almost every week's part causing him in his own judgment to add events to the narrative somewhat too freely' (*The Life and Work of Thomas Hardy*, p. 185).

A different kind of result of serialization was the effective censorship of any passage, or any word, which an editor might deem potentially offensive to any of his readers. This began very early in Hardy's career, when the editor of the *Cornhill Magazine*, in which *Far from the Madding Crowd* was appearing, was alarmed by the fate of Fanny Robin. (Fanny has been seduced by Sergeant Troy and dies in childbirth.) The powerful and daring scene in which Bathsheba forces open Fanny's coffin and finds the dead infant in its mother's arms was something for which the public of the 1870s was simply not ready – at least the magazine-reading public, and at least in the judgment of an editor. The irony of the situation was that the editor in this case, Leslie Stephen (father of Virginia Woolf), was a highly intelligent and perceptive critic and a close friend of Hardy's. (On Stephen's reactions, see also p. 25 above.) As an editor, however, he had no choice but to avoid a situation in which outraged readers might complain loudly or even cancel their subscriptions.

In these ways the effects of serialization on Hardy's novels, as on those of Dickens and others, could be far-reaching in determining what kind of fiction could be written. The pattern of Hardy's career as a novelist is that of a writer anxious to explore serious issues with honesty and directness, and finding the suppressions and repressions caused by editorial interference increasingly irksome. Why he abandoned the novel after *Jude* is a question not readily answered, and certainly not susceptible to a simple answer, but one factor in the situation must have been this sense of frustration.

In the early years of their marriage the Hardys lived in rented homes in London and elsewhere, and Hardy seems to have been in two minds as to the right place to settle. He felt that a professional author needed to be near the centre of the literary world so as to keep in touch with publishers, editors, reviewers and fellow-writers, but he was often ill in London and in any case preferred country life. The result was a compromise. In 1883 he moved into Max Gate in Dorchester, designed by himself and situated within a short distance of his birthplace; but for many years he spent part of each year in London. There are London scenes in many of his novels, and the contrast of town and country is a recurring theme. His return to Dorchester was celebrated in the first novel written after this 'return of the native', *The Mayor of Casterbridge* (1886).

The reception of Hardy's novels was generally mixed, different reviewers – and sometimes the same reviewer – bestowing both praise and blame on different elements in a text. From the outset there were complaints of stylistic awkwardness and excessive allusiveness. These are qualities that some modern critics have viewed very differently: what looks like awkwardness can be regarded as experimentation, individuality and an openness to different varieties of language, while the allusions have been seen as serving a valid purpose by, for instance, linking the limited world of the fiction to a larger world in space and time.

On the other hand, there was often praise for Hardy's handling of his rustic characters, though a few reviewers complained that his true model was Shakespeare's clowns rather than the actual men and women of nineteenth-century rural England. Increasingly as the years passed, however, criticism of Hardy came to focus on moral rather than aesthetic issues. His subjects were sometimes castigated as 'unpleasant', meaning that they dealt frankly with questions of sexuality and other topics that some bourgeois readers preferred not to think about (or at least did not wish their wives and daughters to think about). Especially from *The Woodlanders* (1887) onwards, Hardy probed more and more deeply into the institution of marriage and the problems of marital breakdown. These were far from academic questions where Hardy was concerned, since he and Emma, though they continued to live under the same roof, had become and remained seriously estranged. At the same time they were questions that, in a period when the legal and social status of women was beginning to undergo radical questioning and a degree of change, were very much in the public domain.

As Hardy's later novels became more and more outspoken on issues of love, sex and marriage, hostile reviews and attempts on the part of editors and others to censor his work became more frequent and more extreme. The behaviour of the upper-class philanderer Dr Fitzpiers, in *The Woodlanders*, and the heroine's attempts to escape from a failed marriage in the same novel, caused editorial anxiety, but *Tess of the d'Urbervilles* (1891) was cut much more ruthlessly on its first appearance before the reading public. The firm that had commissioned this novel refused to publish it when they read Hardy's manuscript, which was then refused by other publishers until Hardy cynically set about 'dismembering' it (his own word). All this must have been deeply humiliating, not to say exasperating, to an established writer at the height of his powers. Ironically enough, *Tess* was later to prove a best-seller.

But that was in the future, and it was clear that Hardy could only sell *Tess* as a serial if he made drastic changes and thus seriously damaged the artistic integrity of his novel. The butchery to which *Tess* was subjected consisted of removing two episodes that had given particular offence (the seduction of Tess by Alec, and the 'baptism' and death of her baby), making other omissions, and introducing incidents designed to satisfy the demands of propriety (for example, a fraudulent 'wedding' arranged by Alec to make Tess believe she is married before giving herself to him). A famously absurd example of the changes Hardy found himself compelled to make is the introduction of a wheelbarrow in which Angel Clare conveys the milkmaids across a flooded road: to have carried them in his arms, as Hardy at first described, would have been regarded as unacceptably shocking.

It is important to remember that such changes of Hardy's original intentions in this and other novels were made primarily for the serialized version, and many (though not all) of the original passages were restored when the novel appeared in volume form. (Hardy's reference, in the 1891 Preface to the first edition of *Tess* in book form, to 'slight modifications' is a considerable understatement and surely ironical.) In effect a double standard was operating, on the assumption that a 'family magazine' might easily fall into the hands of the young and innocent, whereas a bound volume or volumes, usually obtained from a circulating library rather than purchased, would be less likely to do so.

Jude the Obscure (1895), nicknamed *Jude the Obscene* and burned by a bishop, was the victim of particularly savage attacks in the press, and the reactions of Hardy, who was always hypersensitive to criticism, probably had something to do with his decision to stop writing fiction. This is by no means the whole story, however, and at least as important is the fact that he was by this time financially secure and could well afford to stop writing for the public and write to please himself. This meant, of course, a return to poetry, and for the remaining thirty or so years of his long life he wrote comparatively little prose but produced an extraordinary body of verse amounting to about a thousand poems.

Hardy thus had two literary careers, as novelist and poet, and so far as publications are concerned the one preceded the other. His fiction-writing career extends from *Desperate Remedies*, published in 1871, to *Jude the Obscure* a quarter of a century later, and he published eight collections of verse, from *Wessex Poems* (1898) to *Winter Words*, which appeared a few months after his death in 1928. (He also published at various times four collections of short stories and an immensely long and ambitious 'epic-drama' about the Napoleonic Wars, *The Dynasts*.) But, as we have seen, he had begun as a poet and had gone on writing poems during the years mainly devoted to fiction, so that the relationship between the two genres is more complex than it might appear.

In a subtler sense, the fiction and the poetry interpenetrate one another in a number of ways. Some of his poems are versions of passages or incidents in novels: 'Midnight on the Great Western', for example, parallels a passage in *Jude the Obscure*, while 'Tess's Lament' and 'We Field-Women' have an obvious relationship to scenes in *Tess*. Other poems, like the fine ballad 'A Trampwoman's Tragedy', show a firm control of narrative art, while incidents in the novels often seem poetically and symbolically conceived. Among English writers Hardy is unique in being both a major poet and a major novelist, but it would be mistaken to regard these as separate careers consecutively pursued. Though it is tempting to say that he was a Victorian novelist and a twentieth-century poet, the second half of this statement is not really borne out by the facts, and his commitment to poetry extended over the astonishing period of some seventy years.

In 1895 Hardy supervised the production of the first collected edition of his writings to date, and for this purpose drew a map illustrating the 'Wessex' in which his fiction is largely set. The relationship between 'Wessex' and the real world as depicted by the Ordnance Survey maps of the period is not a straightforward one. Many of Hardy's descriptions make it perfectly clear what town or village he is referring to: 'Christminster' in *Jude the Obscure* has many of the features of Oxford, with streets, colleges and other buildings thinly disguised under fictitious names. But Hardy reserved the right to take liberties with actuality, and not every locale can be confidently identified with an existing place. Some of the fictitious names strongly suggest their originals (Wintoncester, where Tess is hanged, is obviously the county town of Winchester), while others are less obvious (Melbury, where Sue Bridehead briefly attends a teachers' training college, is based on Salisbury; Casterbridge is closely modelled on Dorchester). Natural features and landmarks such as Stonehenge, on the other hand, are given their real names.

As Hardy's career as a novelist progressed, he became more and more closely identified in the minds of the reading public with a particular region of south-west England, which in turn came to be visited by literary tourists keen on discovering the 'originals' of the fiction. In a sense, though, such a quest is misconceived and even impossible, and Hardy himself was sometimes ironic and gently discouraging towards such enthusiasms. It is not just that the fictional world is something different from a literal representation of reality:

most of Hardy's novels are set in a past that, though not very far distant, is irrecoverable.

One of his qualifications as a writer was to have been born in the right place at the right time. In 1840, Dorset, unlike most of the rest of England (and especially the North and the Midlands), was still largely untouched by the radical changes that transformed nineteenth-century England. The railway, for instance, was not extended to Dorchester until 1847, and Hardy's early childhood was spent in a world that, in outward circumstances, had not changed very dramatically since the time of Shakespeare. His early perceptions were acute and his memory extremely retentive; hence these first impressions of the world remained with him throughout a lifetime that saw more rapid changes than ever before in human history.

Many of his novels are set in a period earlier than the date of composition – not so early as to qualify them as historical novels, but sufficient to convey to their first readers a distinct sense of returning to an earlier generation. Thus *The Mayor of Casterbridge*, written in the 1880s, opens in the 1820s and has its main action set in the 1840s. This was the period of Hardy's childhood and also within the lifetime of older readers, but it was far enough back, given the rapid rate of change in the Victorian period, for contrasts to be made between the old world that was dying and the new one emerging. The central situation of this novel is the displacement of Henchard, with his traditional ways of thinking and doing business, by the 'new man', the scientifically-trained Farfrae. The story dramatizes a kind of speeded-up Darwinian process whereby one species becomes extinct because another is better adapted to survive and flourish. Change is indeed one of Hardy's major themes, especially in his later fiction: in *Tess*, the heroine moves from the timeless world of the dairy farm to the very contemporary, mechanized agriculture of the steam-driven threshing-machine, and the opening sentence of *Jude* announces the first in a series of dislocations that is to dominate that novel ('The school-master was leaving the village ...').

In his later years Hardy's public image changed from that of a figure of controversy and the target of abuse to that of Grand Old Man of English Letters. He was the recipient of many honours, and his international fame led a stream of admirers to beat a path to his door. He continued working into his old age and literally until the day of his death (his last poems were dictated on his deathbed), with the result that his literary career is one of the longest on record. As noted earlier, there are nearly seventy years between the earliest and the latest items in his collected poetical works. Put another way, his career begins in the age of Tennyson and George Eliot and ends in that of the Modernists (he met Virginia Woolf, corresponded with Ezra Pound, and read the poems of D. H. Lawrence as well as befriending many young writers).

Though his work is in some senses strongly local, it attracted the attention of many readers from very different cultures: even in his lifetime he had, for instance, many admirers and translators in Japan, and today the Thomas Hardy Society of Japan still flourishes. Dramatizations of his work were produced on the stage and later for the silent cinema – precursors of the many radio, television and film versions extending up to the present day. These have made his stories, characters and settings familiar to millions who have never read one of his books, and the term 'Wessex', once so unfamiliar, is now used in the names of innumerable businesses and organizations. (At the time of writing, it has very recently been adopted as the title for the earldom conferred on the Queen's youngest son; though Thomas Hardy was not mentioned in newspaper reports of this choice of title, there can be little doubt that it would not have been chosen if the 'Wessex Novels' had never been written.)

In what seems like a paradox, despite its vast and enduring international appeal, Hardy's work has understandably become identified with a certain kind of Englishness. This has sometimes taken the form of treating his books as stimulants to a nostalgic sentimentality about an idealized past, but a careful reading does little to encourage such an approach. Though all his novels are love stories, they take (increasingly in the later stages of his fiction-writing career) a hard look at the problems of relationships between the sexes and, more broadly, at the problems of living in society. Even more broadly, they embody a world-view, sometimes misleadingly referred to as a 'philosophy', that is distinctively Hardyan in its recognition that pain, suffering and injustice are part of the inevitable order of the universe and can only be counteracted by individual acts of 'loving kindness' in a world that does not seem designed for human happiness. Some of the origins of these beliefs, implicit and often explicit in so much of Hardy's work, will be explored in the next chapter.

8

The Context of Hardy's Fiction

The mainstream tradition of the English novel, from Defoe in the early eighteenth century at least until the time of the Modernists some two hundred years later, has always been strongly sociological. In other words, with a few notable exceptions (such as Emily Brontë's *Wuthering Heights*), it has used the conventions of formal realism to present a kind of 'working model' of society, depicting characters in relation to their social roles as well as their inner psychology. Such notable Victorian examples as Thackeray's *Vanity Fair*, Dickens's *Bleak House*, George Eliot's *Middlemarch* and the political novels of Trollope present largely urban settings in which those at different social levels are involved in different kinds of work (or sometimes idleness), and the plots are often driven by tensions arising from social roles or from attempts to transcend the boundaries of class.

Hardy's major fiction follows this tradition, and class issues are of great importance in virtually all his novels. Like Thackeray's Becky Sharp (in *Vanity Fair*) or Dickens's Pip (in *Great Expectations*), such Hardyan characters as Gabriel Oak, Michael Henchard and Jude Fawley show some mobility within the class structure of English society, or at least aspire to such mobility. Work, too, is of great importance in a Hardy novel, and moral distinctions are often made between those who are employed in ways beneficial to the community and those who, like Alec d'Urberville, are not. But whereas the locales of much Victorian fiction are urban, if not metropolitan, in Hardy the town and the city are nearly always at a distance – places that people travel to and return from (though in this as in many other respects *Jude the Obscure* is an exception).

Hardy would have been the last to concede, however, that the obscurity of the settings, or the lack of social pretensions on the part of most of his characters, diminishes the significance of the stories he tells. In the opening chapter of *The Woodlanders* (1887), Hardy suggests that although the tiny community of Little Hintock, in which most of the action takes place, is a remote and secluded spot, 'outside the gates of the world', nevertheless 'from time to time, dramas of a grandeur and unity truly Sophoclean' were enacted there (the reference is to Sophocles, one of the greatest of the Greek tragic dramatists). Hardy's major fiction demonstrates that the novel of provincial and rural life, while dealing at least partly with humble characters, can reach heights of seriousness and even tragedy associated with the greatest productions of world literature. In his 'General Preface' to the important 1912 collected edition of his writings, he points out that the area covered by 'Wessex' is approximately the same as that of the scenes in which the tragedies of Ancient Greece are set.

Hardy's youthful study of Greek drama (he had taught himself Greek) thus left its imprint on his art as a novelist, and his deep interest in poetry and poetic drama also influenced his work in various ways, both at specific points and more pervasively. His writing is often poetic in its use of language: the sensuous and richly symbolical episode in 'the hollow amid the ferns' in *Far from the Madding Crowd* has already been discussed in Chapter 6, and such passages seem ready to compromise between strict realism and the kind of imaginative conception that might have inspired a poem or a scene in one of Shakespeare's romances.

Any account of Hardy as a 'realistic' writer must, therefore, immediately be qualified by recognizing that image and symbol are as important in a novel such as *Tess* as in many works of poetry or poetic drama, and that characters and incidents seem often to be poetically rather than realistically conceived. Consider, for example, the dream-like scene in *The Mayor of Casterbridge* in which Henchard seems to see his own drowned self floating in the river after the skimmington ride. Such passages seem born out of Hardy's fantasies as much as, or more than, his observation of human behaviour.

This enlargement of the provincial or regional novel to incorporate poetic and tragic elements, and the combination of an environment evoked in well-informed detail, with psychological insight, had their most obvious influence upon the early fiction of D. H. Lawrence. It is significant that, at about the time he embarked on his major fiction, Lawrence made a close study of Hardy and, in 1914, actually wrote a short but very personal study of Hardy's fiction (not published until after Lawrence's death). Such novels as *Sons and Lovers* (1913) and *The Rainbow* (1915) show evidence of how what he had learned from Hardy had been adapted to his own highly individual purposes.

Some aspects of the biographical and intellectual context of Hardy's work have already been touched on. In the previous chapter we saw how his training as an architect influenced his work in a number of ways. The hero of his early novel *A Pair of Blue Eyes* is an architect; his minor novel *A Laodicean* makes symbolic use of contrasting styles and fashions in architecture as one of its major themes; and many scenes in the novels pay detailed and knowledgeable attention to buildings, from the description of the Great Barn in *Far from the Madding Crowd* to the episode in *Jude the Obscure* where the stonemason-hero wanders by night among the ancient buildings of 'Christminster' (Oxford).

His architectural training must have helped to sharpen Hardy's naturally keen powers of observation and his sense of spatial relationships, as well as giving him a professional understanding of materials and sites. He also had a strong non-professional interest in the visual arts, especially painting, manifested specifically in numerous references in the fiction to painters and paintings, and generally in what might be called the 'painterly' elements in his descriptions and narratives. The opening of *The Mayor of Casterbridge*, discussed in Chapter 2 above, illustrates both these points. Specifically, the word 'nimbus' points to an implied and somewhat ironic parallel between the group of travellers (Henchard and his wife and child) and the Holy Family of innumerable classical paintings. More generally, the detailed description of Henchard – his face and figure, his dress and manner of walking, the tools he is carrying – constitute the verbal equivalent of a portrait.

Elsewhere Hardy likes to put scenes within a 'frame', supplied, for instance, by a door or window: a little later in the same novel, Susan and Elizabeth-Jane, standing in the street and looking through the hotel window at Henchard as he sits at the public banquet, are like spectators viewing a picture. They are themselves, of course, 'viewed' by the reader, and the motif of 'spying', at times amounting to a kind of voyeurism, is very common in Hardy's narratives. Another example of 'framing' occurs at the beginning of *Jude the Obscure*, when the child looks down a well at a kind of picture within a circular frame.

As a young architect in London, Hardy visited the National Gallery every day during his lunch-hour and made a systematic study of European painting. Later in life he was a regular visitor to the exhibitions at the Royal Academy, and on his European travels visited galleries in Italy and elsewhere. His enthusiasm for the visual arts generated many references to painting and sculpture in his writings, but more important than these is the strongly visual appeal of his narratives. This makes it less surprising that they have been adapted so often and so successfully for visual media such as the cinema. It is worth remembering, too, that most of the novels were, in accordance with standard Victorian practice, accompanied by illustrations on their original appearance, though these were not reproduced when the works appeared in volume form and are not normally included in modern editions.

To turn from the aesthetic to the intellectual context of Hardy's work, something must be said of his response to two issues that were central to Victorian controversy and came to be seen as in opposition to each other: religion and science. Hardy's family were orthodox Christians and he was brought up as a member of the Church of England, attending the village church regularly and acquiring a close knowledge of the Bible and the Book of Common Prayer that finds expression in many ways in his work. Not only are there many quotations from and echoes of Biblical and liturgical language, but characters and situations are sometimes conceived in relation to Biblical parallels. Jude's involvement with Arabella, for instance, is

several times implicitly compared to the ensnarement of Samson by
Delilah in the Old Testament, and Henchard in *The Mayor of Caster-bridge* has much in common with another Old Testament figure, Saul
in the Second Book of Samuel. Hardy also became intimately
acquainted with church music: his family had a long tradition of
playing their instruments in the church band (before the introduction
of the organ), and Hardy's poems in particular contain many allusions
to these memories.

Hardy's religious faith – or at least his attraction to the aesthetic
aspects of the church, including architecture, music, and even such
minor art-forms as the inscriptions on gravestones – were strong
enough for him at one stage to have considered becoming a clergy-man. (This ambition is shared by the last of his protagonists, Jude
Fawley.) As it turned out, though, Hardy's faith was permanently lost,
and his depictions of clergymen (for example, Angel Clare's sancti-monious brothers in *Tess*) are usually unfavourable. His careful study
of the advanced scientific and philosophical ideas of his time, com-bined with his acute awareness of pain and suffering in the world,
made it impossible for him any longer to believe in an all-powerful
and all-loving God.

At the same time it would be wrong to regard Hardy as a militant
or complacent atheist: his self-exclusion from the Christian commu-nity was always a source of regret, even of pain, and there is real
poignancy as well as a characteristic irony in his remark, in his old
age, that he had been looking for God for fifty years, 'and I think, if
he had existed, I would have found him by now'. He insisted to the
end that he was 'churchy', in the sense of enjoying the trappings of
Christian worship (buildings, music, language, ritual): what he simply
could not accept was the doctrines and beliefs. His sense of a God-less world is evident in, for example, the ending of *Tess*, where the
heroine's cruel fate lays bare the absence of love or justice from the
ordering of the universe.

Hardy's scepticism had been reinforced by his readings in nine-teenth-century science, and it is a striking fact that the most influen-tial of all such works, Charles Darwin's *On the Origin of Species*, was
published in 1859, when Hardy was nineteen: precisely, that is, when
he was working towards a system of beliefs to which he could give

intellectual acceptance. Darwin's depiction of a world of ceaseless and merciless struggle to survive, in which the weakest perished, is an informing principle in many of Hardy's fictional situations. Henchard, as we have seen, is a kind of dodo, ill-equipped to cope with the newly emerging world of large-scale, highly professionalized capitalist enterprise, and he dies. Tess's family has had its heyday in the distant past, but, like a threatened species, is near the end of a long process of decline; there is significance in Tess's rape by a son of the new industrialist class (Alec's father has made a fortune in the north of England). Jude, too, with his old-fashioned idealistic notions about learning for its own sake, rather than what the Victorians called 'useful knowledge', cannot survive in an aggressive and competitive world.

From this point of view, *Far from the Madding Crowd*, the earliest of the four novels discussed in the present volume, is markedly different from Hardy's later work. In the rural community it depicts, the church still retains an important place (though the Great Barn, Hardy implies, embodies more enduring values), and the traditional world of skilled craftsmanship represented by Gabriel Oak is not yet threatened by new methods. The figure of the outsider is prominent in Hardy's plots (Farfrae in *The Mayor*, Alec in *Tess*), but the outsider in *Far from the Madding Crowd* is not a representative of the new society that is coming into existence, but another traditional figure, that of the soldier-seducer. And whereas Farfrae triumphs over Henchard, and Tess dies as a result of Alec's invasion of her life, Gabriel Oak is rewarded for his patience and selflessness by ultimately winning the heroine. In the later novels such a happy ending, though reached by way of more than one tragedy, is no longer possible.

Another way of making this point is to say that Hardy had left pastoral behind, even in the modified and less idealized form in which it exists in his earlier work, and had turned to tragedy. This generic change reflects historical changes in Hardy's own lifetime, during which English agriculture was, like Tess Durbeyfield's family, itself in decline. That period saw the completion of the transformation of England from an agrarian to an urban civilization: henceforth most people would live in towns and cities rather than on the land. The world of *Far from the Madding Crowd* is one of shepherds, farm labourers and country craftsmen, with such traditional customs as hiring fairs and harvest suppers, but by the time of *Tess of the d'Urbervilles*, less than twenty years later, that world has been invaded by agricultural machinery which reduces the need for labour and turns such employment as there is into a very different kind of experience.

In *Tess*, indeed, we have the vanishing world and the new world set in contrast. At Talbothays Dairy Farm, Tess is occupied in such traditional tasks as milking and butter-making, but there are reminders of another and very different world outside. In Chapter 30 she and Angel take the milk to the railway station so that it can be rushed to the city in order to supply the breakfast tables of Londoners 'who have never seen a cow' (see pp. 108–13 above). And it is those Londoners rather than Tess who are now representative of the new society that has come into existence.

Such Londoners would of course have formed a large part of Hardy's readership, and there is no doubt that *Far from the Madding Crowd* achieved its great success partly because it opened up to them a world that was intriguingly different (even if 'quaint' and 'old-fashioned'). When Gabriel Oak performs an emergency operation on a sick sheep or struggles heroically to cover the ricks during a storm, this represents for the urban reader an extension of knowledge and experience. This documenting of a way of life that, even as he writes, is in the process of becoming extinct (if it has not already done so) is continued in Hardy's later novels: Henchard in *The Mayor*, for example, is a skilled rural craftsman (a hay-trusser) who retains traditional methods even after he becomes a business man and an employer of labour.

But by the time of *Jude the Obscure*, at the end of Hardy's novel-writing career and near the end of the century, his fictional world has come much closer to the date of composition. Jude begins as a village boy but spends most of his life in towns: the most nomadic of all Hardy's heroes, his restlessness and lack of roots reflect the new civilization that has taken the place of the stable communities of the past. Relationships are fragmented by increased mobility: Arabella goes to Australia, then returns, bringing with her the son Jude does not know or even know of. The links with the past enjoyed by former generations and symbolized by the continuing occupation of a family home, as in the Hardy family, have been broken, and Jude occupies a series of temporary lodgings in different towns.

Although most of the action of most of the novels takes place within the restricted confines of 'Wessex', there are hints of a much larger world. The population of Britain increased rapidly during the nineteenth century, and a large number of people emigrated to distant parts of the world in search of opportunities that the mother country seemed to deny them. In *Tess of the d'Urbervilles*, Angel Clare is one of a group of Dorset farm-workers who emigrate to Brazil in quest of a new life. In *Jude the Obscure*, Arabella and her family go to Australia, only to return when their hopes of easy success are not realized; emphasis is later laid on the fact that the child of Jude and Arabella is a young Australian. And in *The Mayor of Casterbridge* the sailor Newson, who becomes an unofficial husband and father to Susan Henchard and her daughter after the novel's protagonist has (in effect) deserted them, emigrates to North America. One might somewhat cynically suggest that these emigrations are no more than convenient plot-devices to remove from the scene certain characters who need temporarily to be kept at a distance. But they do suggest that Hardy was aware of emigration as one of several factors that contributed to the disintegration of the rural community, and Angel Clare's Brazilian adventure is in fact based fairly closely on contemporary history.

Finally, the linguistic context of Hardy's writing calls for brief comment. The nineteenth century was a great age of linguistic research and dictionary-making, with such enterprises as Joseph Wright's great *English Dialect Dictionary* (1898–1905) providing evidence of an interest in local varieties as well as in the standard language. Hardy knew the Dorset dialect, which was spoken by his father and their neighbours (though his mother, anxious that her children should rise in the world, took pains to eliminate dialect words and expressions from her speech). In his novels, different forms of speech are class-indicators, and the rustic chorus who gather at Warren's Malthouse in *Far from the Madding Crowd* use dialect unselfconsciously, though the intention of the writer, with one eye on his middle-class readers, often seems to be to exploit the eccentricity of such forms of speech for comic purposes.

More problematic is the case of characters caught between two linguistic worlds. Tess has been the recipient of a certain amount of schooling 'under a London-trained mistress', and we learn in Chapter 3 that she 'spoke two languages; the dialect at home, more or less; ordinary English abroad [i.e., outside the family] and to persons of quality'. In a very interesting passage in *The Mayor of Casterbridge* (Chapter 20), the narrator tells us that 'One grievous failing of Elizabeth's was her occasional pretty and picturesque use of dialect worlds – those terrible marks of the beast to the truly genteel.' There is a telling irony in the fact that Henchard, a man of little education whose own speech is often rough, should be driven by social ambition to rebuke the girl bitterly for her use of homely expressions. In these ways Hardy shows an acute awareness, nourished by personal experience, that language, like so much else, is changing rapidly in a world in which familiar habits and landmarks are rapidly being eroded.

9

Samples of Criticism

In this chapter we shall consider extracts from five critical accounts that between them cover a period of some forty years. They also represent different ways of looking at Hardy's fiction, and it is important to insist that with a writer of such richness and complexity it is not a question of one approach being 'right' and another 'wrong', or even of one being 'better' than another (though we may, as individual readers, find particular methods and interpretations more congenial or more helpful than others). Hardy the novelist not only invites but requires a pluralist approach. The critical methods represented here include 'sociological', 'feminist' and 'masculinist' readings, as well as those that make use of historical, biographical and textual information.

Michael Millgate, *Thomas Hardy: His Career as a Novelist* (1971)

This comprehensive and penetrating study appeared near the very beginning of the remarkable boom in Hardy studies that the past thirty years have witnessed. As well as valuable criticism of all of Hardy's fourteen published novels, it offers a chapter on his lost first novel, *The Poor Man and the Lady*, and separate discussions of such topics as 'Politics and Ideas', 'The Evolution of Wessex' and 'Hardy and the Theatre'. The criticism of individual texts is placed within the biographical and bibliographical context of the circumstances of their composition and publication, and there is much information on the intellectual background of Hardy's work and on the writers who influenced him.

Millgate's highly perceptive close readings of the texts are often usefully related to broader generalizations about his fictional method. Thus, in discussing *Far from the Madding Crowd*, he writes:

> It seems to have been Hardy's preferred method to display his princi-
> pal characters in dramatised episodes before introducing them directly
> to the reader, certainly before offering an analysis of their personalities
> or any internal view of their thoughts and feelings: it is thus that
> Bathsheba, Boldwood, and Troy are introduced. Unfortunately,
> Hardy had insufficient faith in his own power to reveal character in
> action, judging it necessary to insert 'set-piece' analyses, unduly long
> and rather inertly abstract, of both Boldwood and Troy at the points
> where they are brought fully into the main narrative stream. He shows
> greater confidence in his dramatic creation of Bathsheba. Although the
> later crises in her life are presented largely in terms of a direct revela-
> tion of what she is thinking and feeling, the early chapters simply offer
> a series of vignettes of her – as tease, as tomboy, as 'mistress of the
> farm', as manager of men – which are allowed to make their own
> impact with the minimum of authorial intrusion.
>
> Some of these episodes take on an almost emblematic quality which
> forces the reader to register them quite consciously as portentous of
> future developments. The most notable of them, Gabriel's view of
> Bathsheba as she sits on the cart surrounded by household impedi-
> menta, admiring herself in the mirror, allows Gabriel himself to draw a
> lesson regarding Bathsheba's vanity, but it also hints at that display of
> femininity in the open air which will cause such damage when Bath-
> sheba takes over Weatherbury Upper Farm and, not least, at that
> element of domesticity in her which Gabriel himself will finally dis-
> cover.... (pp. 82–3)

For Millgate, Hardy is not merely a chronicler of tales based on traditional patterns of narrative but a sophisticated and subtle writer whose work embodies conceptions and attitudes that cannot be reduced to simple formulae. He recognizes, for instance, an element of ambiguity in the presentation of the heroine of *Tess of the d'Urbervilles*:

Tess may be essentially the victim, and we may from an early stage feel that she is doomed, if only because of what myths, ballads and melodramas have taught us to anticipate as the life pattern of seduced country maidens. But Hardy makes clear that Tess herself has choices to make, even if they can only lead her into worse difficulties. She is not entirely helpless in the grip of a mechanistic universe, and a less passive, more self-confident character might have found avenues of escape not discovered by Tess herself. In handling the question of Tess's ultimate responsibility for her most decisive acts – the sexual surrender to Alec, the failure to confess to Angel, the second surrender to Alec, the murder – Hardy achieves an entirely valid ambiguity. He nowhere suggests that Tess is *right* to do these things, and he metes out to her, in terms of mental suffering and the final legalised execution, punishment enough to satisfy the sternest moralist. Yet his compassionate presentation of Tess makes it impossible to make attribution of responsibility co-extensive with assignment of blame, especially since the avoidance of analysis in favour of dramatic and impressionistic techniques forces the reader to an extraordinary degree of participation in Tess's career.   (pp. 279–80)

Arnold Kettle, 'Tess of the d'Urbervilles', in *An Introduction to the English Novel*, Volume 2 (1951)

One important strand of Hardy criticism relates his novels to history, especially the history of rural England in the latter part of the nineteenth century. In this early study, a Marxist critic has interpreted *Tess of the d'Urbervilles* as a kind of parable of the decline and eventual disappearance of the English peasantry, a long-established social and economic group possessed of a distinctive culture:

> The subject of *Tess of the d'Urbervilles* is stated clearly by Hardy to be the fate of a 'pure woman'; in fact it is the destruction of the English peasantry. [The novel] has the quality of a social document. It has even, for all its high-pitched emotional quality, the kind of impersonality that the expression suggests. Its subject is all-pervasive, affecting and determining the nature of every part. It is a novel with a thesis – *roman à thèse* – and the thesis is true.
>
> The thesis is that in the latter half of the [nineteenth] century the disintegration of the peasantry – a process which had its roots deep in

the past – reached its final and tragic stage. With the extension of capitalist farming (farming, that is to say, in which the landowner farms not for sustenance but for profit and in which the land-workers become wage-earners) the old yeoman class of small-holders or peasants, with their traditions of independence and their own native culture, was bound to disappear. The developing forces of history were too strong for them and their way of life. And because that way of life had been proud and deep-rooted its destruction was necessarily painful and tragic. *Tess* is the story and the symbol of its destruction.   (p. 49)

Kettle's reading of *Tess*, in terms of a Marxist view of historical processes, seems to entail a rejection of more traditional interpretations of the novel that (for example) place emphasis on the tragic love story or treat it as a modern reworking of a situation common in old ballads and folk songs. The opening sentence of the above passage shows clearly that his method of argument is along the lines of 'not that, but this'. It can be objected, however, that such a reading is partial and fails to do justice to a many-sided and many-layered work. In the years since Kettle's relatively early essay was published, two generations of critics have collectively illuminated the complexity of Hardy's novel, and to suggest that the 'real' subject of the story is 'the destruction of the English peasantry' rather than the fate of an individual is to risk diminishing and undervaluing Hardy's achievement.

Kettle's view of Tess as the victim of irresistible and inevitable forces may be contrasted with Millgate's perception of her as a character with 'choices to make'. The choices available to the victim of a long-drawn-out historical process must be limited (if not non-existent), and this view of Tess as a symbol of the English peasantry is bound to affect our view of her as a tragic figure, since choice and a degree of responsibility for one's actions and their consequences are of the essence of traditional views of traqedy.

The *Tess* described by Kettle may indeed be a powerful work, but it is a lesser work than the one Hardy wrote. The truth seems to be that characters and incidents in the novel have both an intrinsic and a representative quality: Tess herself is both an individual character with a tragic history and the symbol of an historical process that may also be described as tragic. As this description suggests, 'history' for Hardy is a term with multiple meanings that involve individuals, families and communities as well as classes and nations.

Kettle's approach is, however, valuable in drawing attention to the larger significance of certain elements in the story. It certainly makes sense, for example, to regard the sexual exploitation of Tess by Alec as representing, *among other things*, the 'rape' of the countryside by the new capitalist class (Alec's father, we recall, has made his money in the industrial North). In the following passage, Kettle demonstrates that the opening chapters of the novel are susceptible to being read in terms of the displacement of one class by another:

> In the opening chapters of the novel there is an immediate and insistent emphasis on historical processes, so that from the start the characters are not seen merely as individuals. The discovery by John Durbeyfield of his ancestry is not just an introductory comic scene, a display of quaint 'character'. It states the basic theme of the novel – what the Durbeyfields have been and what they become. The landscape in the second chapter ... is described and given significance almost wholly in terms of history. The 'club-walking' scene, again, is contrasted with the May Day dances of the past and early pagan rites are recalled. Tess is revealed as one of a group, typical ('not handsomer than others'), and in the comparison between her and her mother the differences brought about by historical changes are emphasized. Joan Durbeyfield lives in the peasant folk-lore of the past, Tess has been to a National school. 'When they were together, the Jacobean and the Victorian ages were juxtaposed.' (p. 50)

The comment quoted at the end of this passage shows that the narrator of the novel is capable of anticipating the critic in standing back from the circumstantial detail of the fiction in order to place the characters in a broad historical context. Hardy does this at other points in the narrative: for example, at the end of the 'rape' scene, where the narrator reflects that a kind of rough justice, operating over many centuries, is in operation, since Tess has suffered no more than has been meted out to other girls by her distant ancestors.

Rosemarie Morgan, *Cancelled Words: Rediscovering Thomas Hardy* (1992)

For entirely understandable reasons, Hardy's fiction has in recent years received a considerable amount of attention from feminist critics such as Penny Boumelha, Patricia Ingham and Rosemarie Morgan. The latter's *Cancelled Words* is a close analysis of *Far from the Madding Crowd*, intended to show 'the creative mind at work' through examination of the differences between Hardy's manuscript and the first version of the published novel, issued as a serial in the *Cornhill* magazine. As we have seen already (p. 25), the editor of the magazine, Leslie Stephen, exercised a fairly strict control over Hardy's creative freedom and did not hesitate to urge him, politely but firmly, to delete or at least tone down anything that in Stephen's editorial judgement might cause offence to his readers. Morgan refers to 'the regularity and rigour of his editorial interference in actual practice', in contrast to the suave tones of his correspondence with Hardy, who was later to describe Stephen's criticisms of his work as 'grim and severe'.

In the following passage, Morgan shows how Hardy's presentation of Troy underwent changes in the progress of the novel from manuscript to serial:

> Hardy's first impulse with Troy, in his first conception of him at the manuscript stage of writing, is to colour him not in the flamboyant tones of the seducer-stereotype, but in those Arcadian tones of Greek sensuousness so dear to his own heart. Although Troy has already entered the scene on the periphery, so to speak, first as the soldier incarcerated in Melchester barracks – 'as good as in the county gaol till to-morrow morning', as he tells the lovesick Fanny Robin – and, second, as the bridegroom she accidentally jilts at the altar and who heartlessly spurns her thereafter, it is not until the scene of the fir plantation and his erotic encounter with Bathsheba that Troy takes on the fuller dimension of a rounded, complex character. And it is at this point, in the chapter that follows (Chapter XXV), entitled 'The New Acquaintance Described', that Hardy plunges into Troy's story. Here we learn something of his vices, such as lying like a Cretan and dissembling to women, all of which Hardy renders in tones of light irony and with the kind of uncensorious, wry benevolence we find in

Henry Fielding's *Tom Jones*. This mildly indulgent tone is, however, rather more apparent in the manuscript than in the *Cornhill*. For example, as we are told that 'he never passed the line which divides the spruce vices from the ugly', so we are also told that:

> In his sacrifices to Venus he retained the ancient doctrines of the groves, and introduced vice, not as a lapse, but as a necessary part of the ceremony.

This little touch of pagan licentiousness is silently excised for Stephen's readers in the *Cornhill*.   (p. 23)

One of the interesting points here is that Hardy's excised sentence is carefully worded – so carefully, indeed, that some of his readers would probably have had little idea what he was talking about. But Stephen, as a classical scholar, would have known perfectly well that Venus was in Roman mythology the goddess of love and that 'sacrifices to Venus' was a euphemism for sexual escapades. Similarly, 'the groves' seems to allude to orgiastic ceremonies in the pagan world, perhaps especially those associated with Pan, god of the woods. What the sentence is really saying is that Troy was a philanderer and a hedonist who set no store by conventional Christian morality, and Stephen was aware that at least some of the *Cornhill* readers would catch this meaning. Therefore the sentence had to go.

How important is its loss? Morgan argues that the sentence is not just a passing comment but part of a pattern of allusions that has been constructed within Hardy's text, and that its deletion therefore involves a 'loss of artistic unity':

> ...Ultimately this Venusian reference provides the artistic balance to Hardy's characterisation of Troy in this chapter which relies heavily upon allusions to Greek folklore – from lying Cretans to the refined dissipation of the citizens of Corinth. As an allusion to things youthful and sensual, the excised passage and its reference to the rites of Venus is clearly intended as a prefatory note to the phrase it later justifies, which now runs in the *Cornhill* without qualification:

> He never passed the line which divides the spruce vices from the ugly, and hence, though his morals had hardly been applauded, disapproval of them had frequently been tempered with a smile.

This phrase, standing as it now does without the prefatory justifying reference to Venus and the 'ancient doctrines of the groves', no longer makes any sense. In its present state, sandwiched between Corinthian dissipation and Cretan lying, there is nothing now (aside from the light irony of the allusions) of that soft and sensuous Greek joyousness with which to temper disapproval 'with a smile'.   (p. 25)

The above discussion is focussed on a single example, but Morgan's book demonstrates in detail that Stephen's editorial interference (for which 'censorship' is not too strong a word), however gracefully exerted, made significant changes at many points in Hardy's text. As a result, the novel presented to the first readers of *Far from the Madding Crowd* was not quite the novel that Hardy had written. The case in fact forms a very instructive example of the way in which the artistic and moral intentions of the Victorian novelist could come into collision with the imperatives of editors and publishers as well as with the sensitivities of readers.

Elaine Showalter, 'The Unmanning of the Mayor of Casterbridge', in *Critical Approaches to the Fiction of Thomas Hardy*, ed. Dale Kramer (1979)

This essay by a leading American feminist critic makes very high claims for Hardy's novel as one of the most outstanding works of Victorian fiction, and as 'Shakespearean' in its depiction of the character of the protagonist. The central argument is that Henchard, who starts out as aggressively masculine, learns 'feminine' skills that may also be regarded as part of the equipment of the novelist:

> Hardy gives the fullest nineteenth-century portrait of a man's inner life – his rebellion and his suffering, his loneliness and jealousy, his paranoia and despair, his uncontrollable unconscious. Henchard's efforts, first to deny and divorce his passional self, and ultimately to accept and educate it, involve him in a pilgrimage of 'unmanning' which is a movement towards both self-discovery and tragic vulnerability. . . .

We might read the story of Henchard as a tragic taming of the heroic will, the bending and breaking of his savage male defiance in contest with a stoic female endurance.... Yet this romantic and nostalgic reading would underestimate Hardy's generosity of imagination. Virginia Woolf, one of Hardy's earliest feminist critics, attributed the 'tragic power' of his characters to 'a force within them which cannot be defined, a force of love or of hate, a force which in the men is the cause of rebellion against life, and in the women implies an illimitable capacity for suffering'. In Henchard the forces of male rebellion and female suffering ultimately conjoin; and in this unmanning Hardy achieves a tragic power unequalled in Victorian fiction.... The skills which Henchard struggles finally to learn, skills of observation, attention, sensitivity, and compassion, are also those of the novelist, and they are feminine perhaps, if one contrasts them to the skills of the architect or the statesman. But it is because Hardy dares so fully to acknowledge this side of his own art, to pursue the feminine spirit in his man of character, that his hero, like the great heroines he would create in the 1890s, is more Shakespearean than Victorian.

(The quotation from Virginia Woolf in the above extract is taken from her essay 'The Novels of Thomas Hardy', written just after Hardy's death and included in her collection *The Common Reader: Second Series*, 1932.) One of the interesting features of Showalter's interpretation is that it moves the centre of attention *inside* Henchard's mind and personality, in contrast to the readings that stress the 'rise and fall' pattern of his career and concentrate on the successes and failures in both his business life and his personal relationships.

Some readers may question this critic's identification of certain human 'skills' as specifically feminine or masculine: but it is useful to be reminded that Henchard's nature, as presented by Hardy, is sufficiently complex to embody what appear to be contradictory qualities. Thus, he is shown as having a strongly masculine physical presence and a characteristic manner that can be forthright, aggressive and even bullying; at the same time, though, he is capable of unexpected gentleness, tenderness and vulnerability, as in his impulsive fondness for Donald Farfrae when they first meet.

Richard Dellamora, *Masculine Desire: The Sexual Politics of Victorian Aestheticism* (Chapel Hill, NC, 1990)

Sexuality, an important theme even in Hardy's earlier novels, becomes increasingly prominent in his fiction of the 1880s and 1890s, and by the time we reach *Jude the Obscure* it has become a central concern. Hardy may have originally conceived this work as a tragic study of the failure of a young man to obtain a university education, but it turned into an exploration of often tormented sexual relationships – of men and women prey to what Hardy calls, in his 1895 Preface, 'the strongest passion known to humanity'. In his 'masculinist' discussion of the novel, Richard Dellamora shows that it was 'offensive' to its early readers in more ways than one. He covers familiar ground in reminding us of the hostile reception the work received from reviewers and readers, to the extent that the Establishment (not excluding the Established Church) ganged up on Hardy to prevent the circulation of his book by having it banned by one of the leading subscription libraries patronized by middle-class readers. But Dellamora has new points to make about Jude's isolation from male society – a phenomenon that links his social, emotional and sexual life with his exclusion from a system of higher education reserved for the privileged:

> In 1895... literary scandal attended publication in book form of Thomas Hardy's *Jude the Obscure*. Hardy's writing, like that of [Oscar] Wilde and contemporary feminists, subverted male privilege in marriage. That arbiter of public decency, the *Pall Mall Gazette*, in a review of November 1912 called the novel 'Jude the Obscene' and the London *World* ran its review 'under the title "Hardy the Degenerate"'. Mrs Oliphant reviewed the book as a polemic against marriage. Most spectacularly, Bishop William Walsham How of Wakefield burned the book – then added injury to insult by instigating 'the withdrawal of the novel from W. H. Smith's huge circulating library'.
>
> Hardy's novel was, however, offensive in other ways as well. *Jude the Obscure* is notable for the weakness within it of same-sex bonding – at least for its protagonists, Jude and Sue. Jude has no male friends, he has no entry into the homosocial enclaves to which he is so strongly drawn, especially Oxford. And he repeatedly fails in attempts to achieve a mentor–protégé relationship. His one relationship of the kind, with a

village schoolteacher called Phillotson, proves to be disastrous for both men. And Hardy is mordant about the putative solidarity that exists among working-class males. In focusing on a man whose life is characterized by exclusion from male homosocial ties, Hardy implicitly condemns institutions like Oxford, where a cherished sense of belonging was purchased at the price of a snobbish exclusivity.

Dellamora goes on to argue that Hardy's depiction of Jude's exclusion from such institutions also calls in question accepted notions of the 'gentleman', a concept central to the morality and social cohesiveness of the Victorian ruling class:

> Hardy might also be seen as demythologizing the figure of the gentleman, since in humble, diffuse ways Jude seeks entry into an occupation that would make him a simulacrum of a gentleman. Hardy points out the cruelty to which Jude's naive pursuit of this substitute ambition exposes him. Again not surprisingly, gentlemanly reviewers reacted against the novel. In his life of Hardy, Michael Millgate points out that Hardy was especially aggrieved at 'fellow-members of the Savile Club' who wrote 'hostile reviews' in the 1890s. [Hardy had become a member of the Savile, an exclusive gentleman's club in the West End of London, in 1878 – an outward sign of his relatively new status at that time as a professional man of letters.] Millgate remarks that Hardy's dismay 'reflected his sense, ingrained from childhood, that friendship was inseparable from loyalty, and also his bitter realization that his years of investment in clubbability and *bonhomie* were not, after all, standing him in good stead.' *Jude* repudiates such affiliations; instead, the novel reaffirms Hardy's awareness of himself as an outsider, and asserts his fellowship with someone as estranged as Jude Fawley. (pp. 212–13)

It is interesting to note that Dellamora's new approach to Jude's situation in the novel leads to a familiar conclusion: the reassertion of the novelist's close personal affinity with his protagonist. Hardy repeatedly insisted that the novel was not autobiographical, but the very strength of his insistence is suspicious. There cannot be much doubt that he himself had felt on the pulses much of the experience of his excluded hero.

10

Guide to Further Reading

Autobiography and Biography

Towards the end of his life Hardy wrote an autobiography that was published after his death under the pretence that it was a biography written by his second wife, Florence Emily Hardy. This was a characteristically devious strategy to pre-empt the unwelcome attentions of biographers while maintaining the appearance of objectivity. However, this work, which makes extensive use of quotations from Hardy's diaries and notebooks, is of great interest. It is best consulted in the edition prepared by Michael Millgate, *The Life and Work of Thomas Hardy by Thomas Hardy* (1984), and, since it is a long book, students may wish to concentrate on the sections specially related to the texts they are studying (for example, Part V is on ' "Tess", "Jude", and the End of Prose').

The most accessible short modern biography is James Gibson's *Thomas Hardy* (1996), which can be strongly recommended. For a more detailed account, to be consulted where fuller treatment of specific points is required, see Michael Millgate's *Thomas Hardy: A Biography* (1982). Timothy O'Sullivan's *Thomas Hardy: An Illustrated Biography* (1975) contains many excellent pictures of Hardy, his circle and his world.

Reference

F. B. Pinion's *A Hardy Companion* (1968) and *A Thomas Hardy Dictionary* (1989) are of great value in checking facts and obtaining information on such matters as dialect words and allusions. Timothy Hands's *A Hardy Chronology* (1992) contains a clearly arranged and fully indexed listing of the basic facts of Hardy's life and career. The *Oxford Reader's Companion to Hardy* (2000), edited by Norman Page, is a comprehensive guide, alphabetically arranged, to Hardy's life and work and to the contexts of his writings.

Criticism: General

There has been, especially since the great upsurge in Hardy studies from about 1970, an immense amount of critical writing about Hardy's prose and verse. Some of the most accessible general studies are Douglas Brown's *Thomas Hardy* (1954), Merryn Williams's *A Preface to Hardy* (1976), Norman Page's *Thomas Hardy* (1977), and Robert Langbaum's *Thomas Hardy in Our Time* (1995). Two fine studies devoted to the novels are Michael Millgate's *Thomas Hardy: His Career as a Novelist* (1971) and Ian Gregor's *The Great Web: The Form of Hardy's Major Fiction* (1974). Notable feminist studies include Penny Boumelha's pioneering *Thomas Hardy and Women* (1982); Pamela Jekel's *Thomas Hardy's Heroines* (1986); Rosemarie Morgan's *Women and Sexuality in the Novels of Thomas Hardy* (1988); and Patricia Ingham's *Thomas Hardy* (1989). A stimulating recent study along Marxist lines is Roger Ebbatson's *Thomas Hardy: The Margin of the Unexpressed* (1993). R. G. Cox's *Thomas Hardy: The Critical Heritage* (1970) very usefully assembles important specimens of early reviews, providing insights into the ways in which Hardy's work struck his contemporaries. For a survey of Hardy criticism to 1990, see Charles Lock's *Thomas Hardy* in the Criticism in Focus series (1992).

Criticism: Specific Texts

Far from the Madding Crowd

For understandable reasons, this novel has recently received much attention from feminist critics; for a useful exploration along these lines, see Linda M. Shires's 'Narrative, Gender, and Power in *Far from the Madding Crowd*', in Margaret R. Higonnet (ed.), *The Sense of Sex: Feminist Perspectives on Hardy* (1993).

A more elaborate and controversial discussion of the novel by a feminist critic is Rosemarie Morgan's *Cancelled Words: Rediscovering Thomas Hardy* (1992).

Jude the Obscure

The short study of this novel by Cedric Watts in the Penguin Critical Studies series (1992) considers Marxist, feminist and other approaches. A selection of both older and recent discussions will be found in *Jude the Obscure*, ed. Norman Page, in the Norton Critical Editions series (2nd edition, 1999).

The Mayor of Casterbridge

Douglas Brown's short study, *Thomas Hardy: The Mayor of Casterbridge*, though published as long ago as 1962, is still worth reading. The validity of the 'sociological' approach adopted by Brown is debated in Laurence Lerner's short book *'The Mayor of Casterbridge': Tragedy or Social History?* (1975). More recent studies include Craig Raine's 'Conscious Artistry in *The Mayor of Casterbridge*', in *New Perspectives on Thomas Hardy*, ed. Charles P. C. Pettit (1994).

Tess of the d'Urbervilles

Graham Handley's short study of this novel in the Penguin Critical Studies series (1991) can be recommended. An important discussion of this novel is contained in David Lodge's chapter 'Tess, Nature, and the Voices of Hardy', which looks closely at its polyphonic use of language, in his *Language of Fiction* (1966). A selection of more recent criticism will be found in Peter Widdowson (ed.), *Tess of the d'Urbervilles*, New Casebooks series (1993).

Useful summaries of some of the most important items of criticism on the above novels will be found in the editions in the Everyman Paperbacks series: *Far from the Madding Crowd*, ed. James Gibson (1993); *Jude the Obscure*, ed. Timothy Hands (1995); *The Mayor of Casterbridge*, ed. Pamela Norris (1993); and *Tess of the d'Urbervilles*, ed. James Gibson (1993). These editions have been used as a basis for the quoted extracts in this book.

Index

Austen, Jane, 130

Boumelha, Penny, 188
Brontë, Charlotte, 5, 31
Bronte, Emily, 5, 174

Coleridge, Samuel Taylor, 81
Collins, Wilkie, 5
Conrad, Joseph, 20, 166
Cowper, William, 89

Darwin, Charles, 82, 155, 178–9
Dellamora, Richard, 192–3
Dickens, Charles, 4, 5, 30–1, 54, 174

Eliot, George, 4, 21

Gifford, Emma: *see* Hardy, Emma
Giotto, 55
Gray, Thomas, 26–7, 164

Hardy, Emma, 165
Hardy, Jemima, 151
Hardy, Thomas,
  works by:
  Desperate Remedies, 163–4
  Dynasts, The, 169
  Far from the Madding Crowd, 21–7, 40–5, 71–4, 85–91, 122–7, 131–6, 164, 165
  Jude the Obscure, 11–16, 45–51, 65–71, 96–100, 113–17, 136–42, 169

Mayor of Casterbridge, The, 6–11, 32–40, 74–8, 100–5, 117–22, 142–7, 162, 165
Pair of Blue Eyes, A, 176
Poor Man and the Lady, The, 163
Return of the Native, The, 32, 55, 56, 108
Tess of the d'Urbervilles, 16–21, 51–6, 60–5, 91–5, 108–13, 147–53, 163, 168–9
Trumpet-Major, The, 165
Two on a Tower, 165
Under the Greenwood Tree, 31, 130, 131
The Woodlanders, 56, 168, 175
Hardy, Thomas (the elder), 151
Hemingway, Ernest, 30
Homer, 141

Ingham, Patricia, 188

Kettle, Arnold, 185–7

Larkin, Philip, 88
Lawrence, D. H., 130, 172, 176

Martin, Julia Augusta, 162
Millgate, Michael, 183–5
Milton, John, 55
Morgan, Rosemarie, 188–90
Moule, Horace, 162

Pound, Ezra, 172

Rembrandt, 104
Ruskin, John, 63

Shakespeare, William, 49, 95, 167
Showalter, Elaine, 190–1
Sophocles, 175
Stephen, Leslie, 25, 166, 188–90

Tennyson, Alfred, 59
Thackeray, W. M., 35, 174

Winterbottom, Michael, 13
Woolf, Virginia, 30, 172, 191
Wordsworth, William, 59, 171
Wright, Joseph, 181